In Search of a Boy Named Chester

A gift to my father for his 100ᵗʰ birthday

FORD S. WORTHY

ISBN: 979-8-9995577-9-7 (print)
ISBN: 979-8-9995577-0-4 (ebook)

InSearchOfChester.com

Dedicated to my father

Ensign Ford S. Worthy, Jr., above left, as he would have appeared to Chester's mother when he met her and Chester at the San Francisco airport in late November 1945. After his return from the war, knowing he would soon be headed for home leave, he cut off the beard he had worn aboard the *USS Lackawanna* and went straight to a photographer's studio to have this photo taken, sometime between October 24 and November 6. At right, FSW Jr. at a party celebrating his 99th birthday on September 22, 2023. (Photo by Marjorie H. Worthy)

1

A SPECIAL BIRTHDAY GIFT

Posted on Facebook June 18, 2024

My father is about to turn 100 – and the gift I'd like to give him depends on your help.

For the past 79 years, my father has wondered whatever became of Chester Park, a precocious boy of around 10 years old, who in a gesture of patriotism by his mother was placed in the care of a complete stranger (my then-21-year-old father) for a flight from San Francisco to Omaha, Nebraska where the boy's grandmother was supposed to pick him up.

Here's the rest of the story – for you to share, and for your friends to share, until someone, somewhere, can tell my father what became of Chester Park.

The story begins in November 1945, in San Francisco. The war had ended a few months earlier with Japan's surrender in Tokyo Bay on September 2. My father, an ensign in the Navy, had served on an oil tanker in the Pacific, and in the weeks since V-J Day, he, along with thousands and thousands of other service members, had returned to the United States via the port of San Francisco, where they were welcomed and celebrated as war heroes. Large and small acts of appreciation were happening daily throughout the city.

My father had been granted a one-week leave before his next assignment – precious little time to make his way 3,000 miles across the country to his home in a small town in eastern North Carolina. He was homesick for his parents and his girlfriend, even for a brief visit. But there was a problem: Hordes of other returning servicemen also wanted to get home – and every bus, car, train, and plane headed out of San Francisco was booked solid for the next 30 days.

The fiancée of my father's shipmate worked for one of the airlines and told Dad that if he would go to the airport, she would find him a ticket out of San Francisco. He waited at the airport for several hours, and finally he was called over to meet Mrs. Park, who was due to depart shortly on a flight to Omaha. Mrs. Park volunteered to give up her seat to my father, who must have looked pretty snappy in his crisp Navy dress uniform. It was her way of thanking this young sailor for defending her country. There was one condition: Dad would need to accompany her young son, Chester, and be responsible for delivering Chester safely to her mother, who would be waiting for him at the Omaha airport.

My father told Mrs. Park they had a deal.

I'll let Dad take it from here – it's his story, after all:

"Chester was a young fellow – probably around 10, he could have been 9, he might have been 11. It was clear he knew a lot about planes. I'm not sure what kind of plane we were on – it could have been a C-54. Chester started right away identifying things like the ailerons and other parts of the plane. I was shocked by how much he knew.

"My memory is that we made a stop somewhere – Las Vegas, possibly – and I got off the plane to get a drink at the airport bar. I told Chester to stay on the plane, and I would be right back. When I got back on, he was having a scrap with the stewardess. I heard him tell the stewardess that she better watch out, because his daddy would be back soon. I said to myself, 'Oh, no, his mother must have told him to tell whoever asks that I'm his daddy.'

"When we arrived in Omaha, Chester and I started looking for his grandparents. There was absolutely nobody who looked like they could be his grandparents. Finally, the terminal had emptied out. Still no grandparents. I began to wonder if someone was playing a trick on me – maybe Mrs. Park was trying to find a home for that boy.

"Now, the next leg of my trip home was in two hours. I had two hours to figure out what to do with Chester. I can still remember debating in my mind, what should I do? Should I leave the boy with a policeman? Should I leave him with the airline? Should I take him with me? If I had had a cellphone, I would have called my own mother and asked her what to do. The one thing I knew for certain was that when my plane took off, I was going to be on it. I was going to leave when that plane took off. The question was: Would Chester be on it with me?

"I agonized about what to do, and I had just made the decision that I was going to take Chester with me.

"I had promised his mother that I would be responsible for him.

"And just as we were getting ready to board the next plane, here come his grandparents! I was never so relieved in my life."

For 79 years my father has imagined how his life might have changed if no one had shown up to claim Chester. He's also wondered how Chester's life turned out. He's tried looking him up in old San Francisco and Omaha phone books and city directories, but he's never tried Facebook.

So ... Facebook, do your thing! Help my father find out whatever became of Chester Park?

2

NEW CLUES IN THE SEARCH FOR CHESTER

Posted on July 1, 2024

Two weeks ago I enlisted your help in tracking down Chester Park, a young boy who, in November 1945, was placed in the care of my father, a complete stranger newly returned from Navy service in the Pacific, on a flight from San Francisco to Omaha.

For almost 79 years, my dad has wondered whatever became of that boy, who knew about ailerons and other parts of an airplane like the back of his hand and who, even before they landed in Omaha, was calling my father "Daddy."

Since that first post, I've heard from hundreds of you – many of you sending early birthday wishes to Dad, who will turn 100 on September 22 – but I haven't yet found Chester.

And that's my goal: as a birthday gift to my father, to satisfy his decades-long curiosity about how Chester turned out.

So ... I'm sharing this update, with some new details that may help the Internet sleuths among you solve this challenge.

After posting the original story, I had a hunch: Perhaps there might be clues buried within a voluminous trove of letters between my father and his parents and friends – correspondence sent and received between 1941 and 1946. Dad kept all the letters he received during those years, and his mother and father kept his letters to them; in all, there are more than 600 letters, or about one letter for every three days over a five-year period. As in so many other ways, the world back then was a very different place when it came to communicating with one another.

What I was hoping to find was the name of Dad's shipmate's fiancée, who worked for an airline and, as Dad recalled, was the person who offered to pull some strings to help him get on a flight out of San Francisco. I not only came up with her name, I discovered a letter written to her by my father (but, curiously, never mailed). Dated December 10, 1945, it was addressed to: Miss Sarah M. Liggett, 291 Geary Street, San Francisco, California. Dad wrote the letter from the Navy base in Norfolk, Virginia, where he had been temporarily assigned

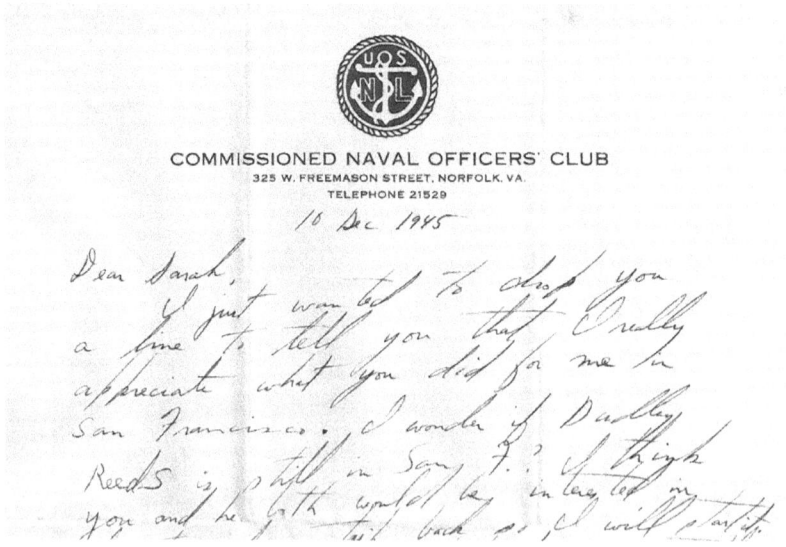

The beginning of a letter dated December 10, 1945, from FSW Jr. to Sarah Liggett, thanking her for helping him get a flight out of San Francisco.

after his home leave in North Carolina. "Dear Sarah," it began, "I just wanted to drop you a line to tell you that I really appreciate what you did for me in San Francisco. ... I think you and [Dudley, her soon-to-be husband] would be interested in the story of my trip back, so I will start it."

As I was reading this yellowed, old letter, the distinctive slant of my father's penmanship so familiar to me, something that Tennessee Williams once wrote came to mind – something about memory taking poetic license. Did Chester's mother really give up her seat to honor a dashing young sailor so he could get back home for an all-too-brief home leave right after the end of the long war? Or did my father do her a favor by volunteering to chaperone her young son for a sudden trip to see her mother in Omaha?

Here's how Dad described the situation in his letter to Sarah:

> "So [the baggage lady] got me on the 5:30 plane. When she put me on she asked if I would do a favor for a friend of hers & an employee of United Airlines. I said sure so she introduced me to a lady about 30 who told me she was going to the hospital & she was divorced & had to send her little son to visit her mother in Omaha"

The letter ends there. Full stop. Not even a perfunctory period after the word "Omaha". Why it was never finished and apparently never sent, my father cannot remember.

These new details, though, should help us find out what became of Chester.

Dad is certain that the boy's first name was Chester, a bit less certain that his last name was Park. We now know, however, that in November 1945, my father was asked by a woman to deliver her young son to her mother in Omaha, Nebraska; her mother (Chester's grandmother) would be waiting for them at the airport there. To my father's eyes, the woman appeared to be "about 30" and her son, Chester, seemed to be around 10 or 11. Chester's mother was divorced. And for unknown reasons, she was planning to go to the hospital after placing Chester in my father's care and seeing him off to Omaha.

The response to my original post has been heartwarming. Hundreds of people have "Liked," or commented on, or shared it on Facebook, and it inspired a lot of you to send early birthday wishes to my father. Many of you have taken the time to scour sources like the U.S. Census and other online records, including Ancestry, to help me zero in on Chester.

For a day or two last week, I thought I might have located Chester. This Chester Park was born in 1933 and would have been 11 in 1945 – a match with my father's recollection. In November of that same year, his mother would have been 33. According to this Chester's daughter, with whom I exchanged several email messages, this boy's grandparents lived in Omaha – another match. When he grew up, this Chester Park became a Marine who served in the Korean and Vietnam wars, and his later hobby as a ham radio operator who could fix most anything synced up nicely with the whip-smart kid who could identify ailerons and other features of an airplane. "We lost him in 2007," his daughter wrote me, "otherwise he would be the first to raise a glass to a fellow veteran on this milestone birthday."

Alas, the new information I uncovered after the original Facebook post rules out this Chester. Unlike the boy in my father's story, this

Chester's parents never divorced.

I've also been able to eliminate several other Chester Parks.

Meanwhile, some intriguing Internet crumbs are now leading my father and me down a path that could conceivably end not with a Chester *Park*, but with a Chester by a different last name.

So, please keep searching – and sharing.

3

WHAT ARE THE ODDS?

Posted on July 12, 2024

W hat are the odds we will find him – the Chester, that is, whose story is so indelibly etched in my father's memory of November 1945?

When I first put out the call on Facebook a few weeks ago, we knew that, to my father's eye, the boy looked to be about 10 then, give or take; his mother looked to be around 30. Also lodged in Dad's mind for all these years was the boy's name: Chester Park. We had a few other details to go on, too: Chester's mother was divorced, and his maternal grandmother lived in Omaha, Nebraska, where she was supposed to pick up Chester at the airport when he arrived on the flight from San Francisco. We also know that my father was introduced to Chester's mother by an employee of United Airlines – raising the possibility, given the circumstances, that Chester's mother may also have worked for United.

My father has wondered forever what became of that little boy, whose mother had entrusted him to a complete stranger, with the expectation that the stranger would deliver the boy safely to his grandmother in Omaha. For my father, who had turned 21 just weeks earlier, the stress and strain of this responsibility was overwhelming. "What have I gotten myself into?" he asked himself when Chester began calling him "Daddy?"

When I promised Dad that I would try, as a gift for his 100th birthday, to find out whatever became of Chester, the odds of success seemed daunting. From a few forays into family history, I knew a little bit about apps like Ancestry, which open the door to massive repositories of searchable data – from U.S. Census records to newspapers to vital statistics about births, marriages, divorces and deaths. Since beginning this deep dive, I've discovered an industry of opportunities to help people learn about their past or make distant connections through online school yearbooks, voter registration records, city directories, family trees, corporate alumni associations, and many, many more stores of information.

Even with all these powerful data-dredging tools, I know there are bound to be a lot of Chester Parks out there. And Dad's Chester, if in fact he is alive today, would be roughly 90 – a nonagenarian just like my father. Discovering what happened to him, I realize, likely means tracking down Chester's siblings or children or grandchildren or perhaps a neighbor or co-worker for whom the story and its biographical particularities ring a bell. And then, supposing I do get a plausible hit, would they be willing to engage with me – a stranger, myself, contacting them out of the blue, like so many catfishers and scamsters up to no good on the Internet? I wouldn't blame Chester's descendants for giving me the silent treatment. I wouldn't blame them a bit.

Still, I want to quantify what I'm up against. What are the odds? How many people might check all the boxes? How many boys named

Chester were about 10 years old in 1945, whose mother was approximately 30 years old, was divorced, and whose own mother lived in Omaha, Nebraska?

With apologies to the statisticians, here's my best effort to make sense of the odds of finding my father's Chester.

The name Chester has been on a downward trend for more than 100 years. In 2023 Chester was the 1,739th most popular first name among baby boys born in the United States; only 94 boys named Chester were born that year.

But the name Chester used to be far more common. For example, more cities in the United States are named Chester than all but Franklin, Clinton, Madison and Washington. And as a first name for people, Chester ranked No. 53 in 1919. The Social Security Administration processed Social Security card applications for 1,432 males named Chester who were born in 1935, the year our Chester was born if he was 10 when he took that ride with my father.

My father guesstimated that his Chester was 10, but more realistically let's assume Chester was born sometime between 1933 and 1937. Five years of baby Chesters born during that time span means that our search is for one of approximately 7,160 Chesters who were between the ages of 8 and 12 in 1945. To err on the conservative side, I rounded that up to 8,000 to acknowledge the fact that a lot of people never applied for a Social Security card if they were born before 1937; that was the year the U.S. Supreme Court upheld the constitutionality of the Social Security Act.

How many Chesters in our target group had mothers who, in 1945, looked to be "around 30"? For present purposes, I've assumed that Chester's mother was between the ages of 25 and 35 when my father briefly encountered her. In turn, if Chester was between 8 and 12 years old at that time, his mother could have been as young as 13 and as old as 27 when he was born. If I've correctly interpreted data from the National Center for Health Statistics for the mid-1930s, it appears that women in that age cohort then accounted for roughly half of all births in the U.S. That would mean about 50% of the 8,000 Chesters we began with had mothers who were in the right age range. In one fell swoop our target group has been cut in two, from 8,000 Chesters to a mere 4,000 Chesters.

When it comes to applying the divorce filter, there are far more complexities than I'm qualified to sort through. Divorce rates can be notoriously difficult to measure, even among experts. The probability of being a divorced woman is obviously different than the probability of being the child of a divorced woman, and the likelihood of being the child of a divorced 25- to 35-year-old woman is different than the likelihood of being an 8- to 12-year-old child of a divorced woman who's 25 or older but no older than 35. And so on …

I'm sure some demographer or genealogist can maneuver amongst all these nuances and come up with a precise number for our situation, but in the meantime I'm going to use a statistic published by the National Center for Family and Marriage Research at Bowling Green State University. In 1945, among all women who had ever been married, perhaps 5% were either separated or divorced at that time. (Over the past 80 years, the percentage has risen to over 20%.) This measure, which includes women who have children and those who do not, is not exactly on point, but it will have to do until an expert steps up with a better approach. Multiplying 5% times our 4,000 remaining possibilities yields just 200 8- to 12-year-old boys named Chester whose mothers, in 1945, were both divorced and between 25 and 35 years old.

Someone among these 200 Chesters is very possibly, and maybe even likely, my father's Chester. Except we don't have to stop there: At the pivotal moment in my father's story – November 1945 – you no doubt recall that Chester's grandmother (his mother's mother) lived in Omaha, Nebraska; or, to be more precise, it was at the Omaha airport where she rendezvoused with my father and her grandson. Geographically and by population, Omaha (1945 population: 240,000) was not far from the center of the 48 states that then comprised the United States; it was an emerging stopover hub for the surging airline industry. Roughly speaking: If the maternal grandmothers of all 200 of these Chesters were spread out evenly across the country and across its post-war population of 133 million people – measured either by geography or by population – you would expect to find more than one of them and less than two of them in the entire state of Nebraska (1945 population: 1.2 million).

Did I say the odds of success were daunting?! By my crude calculus, the probabilities suggest that there is less than one person for whom I can expect to check all the boxes. A boy named Chester, between the ages of 8 and 12 in 1945. A divorced mother then 25 to 35 years old. A maternal grandmother living in Omaha.

And how much rarer still would this grain of sand in the desert become if we added the condition that Chester's mother worked for United Airlines? I'm not going to go there, partly because I know the answer becomes infinitesimal, but mainly because my father's description of the airport encounter reveals only that he was introduced to Chester's mother by a United employee; however awkward the syntax in his letter to Sarah Liggett, he never says anything about who

Chester's mother may have worked for, or if she worked for anyone.

Still, one wonders why United was apparently willing to permit a young boy to be consigned to the care of an unrelated passenger – unless, perhaps, Chester's mother was a fellow United employee, whose child would naturally be looked after during the flight by her United colleagues. That might explain a lot. So, please let me know if you have ideas about how to verify whether Chester's mother was or was not employed by United Airlines. My original post is currently circulating on a private Facebook group devoted to helping United employees find "long lost friends and coworkers," but the company's corporate office has not responded to my inquiries.

The good news about these probabilities is that if this search comes up with someone who checks all these boxes, I, at least, will be persuaded that I've found my father's Chester!

More good news is that my father and I have identified a reasonably promising prospect. There's still a great deal more digging to do – and this lead, like others, may not pan out.

4

THE GHOST OF
MARY E. JOHNSTON

Posted on July 20, 2024

My father has wondered endlessly all these years whatever became of that precocious boy. As a gift to my father, who will celebrate his 100th birthday in two months, I promised to try to answer that question. Over the past month, I've written about my search in three Facebook posts, which I'm now calling chapters.

I *may* have found him.

Dad agrees, sort of – but I can tell he still harbors a little doubt – mostly because he was so sure the boy's name was Chester *Park*.

I'm not ready to make any definitive declarations. Not yet anyway. And the reason is: the ghost of a woman named Mary E. Johnston, who I'm quite sure is looking over my shoulder even now, some 37 years after her retirement as chief of reporters for *Fortune* magazine. Mary, one of the most important people in my entire life, passed away in 1989.

Here, it's necessary to take a quick detour from my father's story and shift over to my story for a moment. Mary Johnston was a legendary figure at Time Inc. For decades she was responsible for hiring and training researchers and reporters for *Fortune*, which was part of Time

Inc. and used to be a big deal in the world of journalism. I was introduced to Mary in 1979, in New York, shortly after graduating from
college. My purpose for being in New York was to interview with several Big Eight accounting firms, with the hope that one might hire me
for a job in Paris. I wasn't really interested in accounting, but I thought
it could be helpful for eventually landing the job I first began dream-
ing about as a young teenager: writing for *Fortune*. In the meantime, it
might be fun, I thought, to learn some French and experience the City
of Light.

I told Mary Johnston I planned to come back two years later – flu-
ent in French and with a CPA certificate in hand – and that I hoped to

Mary E. Johnston, *Fortune* magazine's legendary chief of
reporters, with me and my bride (Allison) at our wedding,
December 1, 1984.

persuade her that I was worthy of a position at *Fortune*. To my surprise, she called me two weeks later to offer me a job – and she changed the trajectory of my life. I started off clipping newspapers and magazines and delivering the clippings to my new colleagues, and later I moved into the researcher ranks and I eventually became a writer for *Fortune*. (It's also where I met my future wife.) From Mary I learned what it meant to be able to say, definitively, that something was true – or not. When *Fortune* published something, it had to be exhaustively evaluated and documented. And if we didn't have the necessary sourcing, we didn't publish it.

Which brings me back to Chester. I think I've found my father's Chester, but certainly not by Mary Johnston's standards. While I continue trying to document the case for one particular Chester – with help, by the way, from people throughout the country – let me tell you how I got to this point.

When I put up the first post asking for your help in locating Chester Park (or more likely, his presumed descendants), I assumed that I would hear from a few real-life friends who might tap into Ancestry and point me towards some possible prospects. My plan was to follow up later with a second post basically reporting that it was unrealistic to expect that I could find the young boy who was entrusted by his mother to my father in November 1945. Their unlikely encounter happened a long time ago, and there were simply too many possibilities to run down. My father might profess disappointment, but he would know that I had tried – and he would have enjoyed the hunt. That was how I saw the story ending.

After the original post there was a burst of suggestions and leads from friends and from a lot of people I didn't know, urging me to scrutinize Chester Y. Park in Hustontown, Pennsylvania, and Leonard Chester Park in Kern County, California, and Chester E. Park in Bruning, Nebraska, among others by that name. I carefully assessed the case for each and every one of these Chester Parks, even as Internet search engines tried, doggedly, to steer me to Chester Park – not the person, but the leafy kind of park – in Duluth, Minnesota, or Anchorage, Alaska, or to eponymous centers of learning like P.S. 62 Chester Park in Queens, New York.

One Chester Park intrigued me for a while. He was born in 1933, and his grandparents lived in a small town in Kansas called Greenleaf, close enough to Omaha to imagine that they might have driven 150 miles north to pick up their grandson from the airport. It was only after several back-and-forth interactions with this Chester's daughter, who lives in California, that she and I both realized, to our disappointment, that her father was not my father's Chester. She wrote me a lovely note that captured the spirit of what a journey like this can be all about: The connections one makes along the way can be reward enough. This daughter of that Chester Park understood the essence of why my father's story and my search appear to be striking such a chord for so many people.

After several weeks of searching intensely – reaching out to scores of other people and scouring U.S. Census records and a multitude of other sources – I decided that in order to have a real chance of finding Chester, I needed to narrow the field.

But before I narrowed the field, I needed to expand it.

I wasn't making much progress in searching for Chester Park, the name that has been preserved in my father's memory for 79 years. Perhaps I needed to consider the possibility that the boy's name was not Chester Park after all.

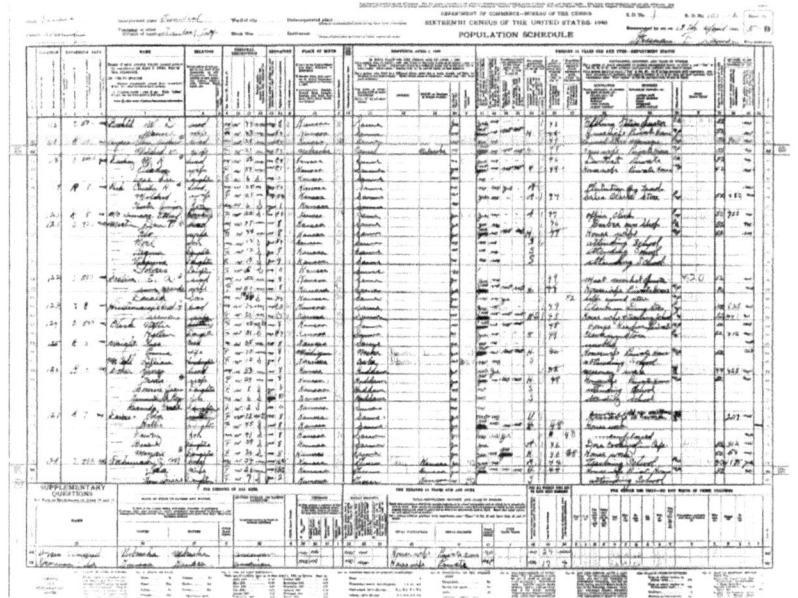

The search for Chester began with the 1940 Census of the United States, when he would have been approximately 5 or 6 years old. Enumerators went door to door to obtain information about each of the country's households, recording by hand the answers to more than 30 questions.

I decided to assume that my father's memory may have been only half right: that I should be looking for a *Chester* or a *Park*, but not necessarily a Chester Park.

If my father could be only half right, it's impossible for me to believe he would forget the name Chester, a name that once was fairly popular but which, to my ear at least, has become more unique, even more unforgettable, as its usage has declined. In 2023 Chester was the 1,739th most popular name for baby boys born in the United States. By comparison, the name Park seems far less memorable. So I decided to assume that the boy's *first* name was Chester, but that his *last* name may have been something other than Park.

My search quickly picked up steam. Whereas before there had

been just a few Chester Parks to investigate, I suddenly had thousands of Chesters to analyze. A search of the 1940 U.S. Census, for example, yielded 7,419 Chesters who were born in either 1933, 1934, 1935, 1936 or 1937, meaning they would have been between 8 and 12 in 1945, the age range I was using as a proxy for my father's recollection that his Chester was around 10 years old in 1945.

At first glance this result seemed insurmountable. But for me, it offered a welcome new angle.

In the telling and retelling of my father's story about Chester, one constant has always been that Chester's grandmother – his mother's mother – picked him up at the airport in Omaha. As I considered this huge batch of Chesters, I learned something about geographic mobility among Americans: While mobility has risen over the years, in 1940 more than three-fourths of U.S.-born Americans lived in the same state in which they were born. Given the tendency of folks not to move around so much, it would be unsurprising if Chester's mother had been born in Nebraska, the same state where her mother presumably lived; and if Chester's mother was born in Nebraska (and perhaps in Omaha, Nebraska) there was a decent chance, it seemed to me, that Chester may have been born there, too.

A similar conjecture could be made about the only other location with which we know Chester was definitely connected: California. It was in San Francisco, at the airport there, where Chester's mother asked my father to be responsible for delivering her young son to her mother in Omaha. Whether mother and son lived in San Francisco, or somewhere in the region, we do not know; but certain other details and inferences point in that direction. For example, when Chester's mother turned her son over to my father, she appears to have been on her way, for completely unknown reasons, to a hospital – an indication, perhaps, that she may have lived within reasonable proximity of the airport. And then there is that fuzzy, potential connection between Chester's mother and United Airlines, which had a major presence in California.

It seemed obvious, therefore, that I should focus first on boys in Chester's age group who were born either in California or Nebraska. When I applied this criteria against the 1940 Census, those 7,419 Chesters I mentioned a few paragraphs ago became just 221 Chesters – 45 born in Nebraska and 176 born in California. These numbers revealed something else: The name Chester was far more common in certain parts of the country than others. In the mid-1930s boy babies in both Nebraska and California accounted for a lower share of all Chesters compared with their respective proportion of the total U.S. population. By comparison, the proportion of all Chesters born in Kentucky, say, was triple that of Kentucky's share of the U.S. population.

As I began to drill down on each of the Chesters in this new, more manageable, group, the mobility data on Americans' tendency, at that time, to stay close to home suggested I would find that the vast majority of all Chesters still lived in the same state in which they were born. In our case, given the two locations with which our Chester was definitely associated, that would be either California or Nebraska. It seemed unlikely that many would have easily observable connections to both California and Nebraska. That also meant, though, that any outliers – Chesters born in Nebraska, say, who by 1945 lived in California, or vice versa – might be easy to spot!

This was exactly what I found – and more.

In Chapter 5 this inspiration will lead me to a boy named Chester, who was 11-and-a-half-years old in November 1945; this Chester's mother, then 34 years old, was divorced and living (with Chester) on the Oakland side of San Francisco Bay; and her mother (Chester's grandmother) lived in Omaha, about six miles from what was then called the American Legion Municipal Airport.

5

A STORY WITHIN A STORY

Posted on July 29, 2024

"How many more chapters in the Chester story," a friend asked me recently?

The truth is, I don't have any idea where this story will take me, or how or when it will end. I originally thought it would be told in two posts – a poignant, patriotic beginning and an unresolved, I-gave-it-my-best-shot ending. Last week I believed I was hot on the trail, and a conclusion seemed close on the horizon. But I'm realizing, as I continue the search for the boy my father unexpectedly encountered 79 years ago in an airport in San Francisco, that this is more than a detective story. It's a story with many strands – different themes that touch on memory, family, patriotism and small towns, data and privacy, and trust – and some of these stories within the main story also deserve to be told.

Every Monday night I have dinner with my father at his home in Raleigh, North Carolina. Monday is my night, and my three sisters each have their nights. When my father tells others about his dinner schedule, he says he wishes he had had three more children to cover the full week.

FSW Jr. mailed this postcard to his sister the day after his ship returned from the Pacific on October 24, 1945. Japan's formal surrender had occurred seven weeks earlier, on September 2, when Adm. Chester W. Nimitz, in a ceremony on the *USS Missouri* in Tokyo Bay, signed the Japanese Instrument of Surrender on behalf of the United States.

I usually show up around 4:30 or 5, prepare a simple dinner for the two of us, and then, around 10 or often later, head back to my home 30 miles away. I see him at other times, of course, but over the past few years these five or six hours have become more special than I could ever have imagined. It's a time for me to tell him not only about what's going on in my life, but how I'm feeling about what's going on. It's a time for him to tell me the same about whatever's on his mind. No interruptions, no distractions. Just him and me, one on one – together at a time in our lives when neither of us is rushed; we can savor even the smallest moments.

It's frequently a time for him to tell – or retell – stories about his life. Sometimes these are stories that he hopes will be remembered, but mainly he tells his stories simply because he enjoys telling them.

On a recent Monday night, he told me a story that revealed how I fit into the story about Chester.

Those of you who've followed these posts, or "chapters," as I'm now calling them, have probably noted all the references to November 1945. That was the point in time that my father placed his encounter with Chester, who was a young boy around 10 years old when his mother entrusted him to a total stranger (my father) for a flight from San Francisco to Omaha.

The November 1945 date fit with what I thought I knew: Years ago I had come across a faded picture postcard of the Golden Gate Bridge (it's shown on the opposite page) with a ship passing beneath the center span. It was addressed to Dad's sister (my aunt). The only message was written, in his handwriting, on the front of the card:

"AO-40"

"0943"

"24 October 1945"

AO-40 was the Navy's designation for "Auxiliary Oiler," the class of oil tanker Dad served on in the Pacific.

0943 was the exact time of day his ship steamed into San Francisco Bay; and

24 October 1945 – that was the day of his return home to his country, safe and sound, after the end of World War II.

Whimsically, but meaningfully, my father had traced over the photo of the ship, adding a smokestack, a signal bridge, and a chain locker to transform the silhouette of that ship into his own, the *USS Lackawanna*. It gives me goosebumps to imagine Dad's oiler entering San Francisco Bay, with its crew of more than 200 singing "San Francisco, open your golden gate" and the Homeward Bound pennant fluttering above them – one white star against a blue field for every officer, followed by one linear foot of red over white for every enlisted man. The card was postmarked the very next day: San Francisco, California, 1130 AM, October 25th, 1945. There would be no forgetting that day or date.

Dad's trip with Chester, therefore, occurred no earlier than October 24, and I knew from a different letter that it occurred no later than December 10, 1945.

On more than a few Monday nights since I began this quest, Dad and I have gone over every memory he can summon up about this story. But as we talked over dinner last week, it occurred to me that I had never asked him, point blank, if he remembered the exact date of the flight from San Francisco to Omaha. Knowing the exact date could be valuable, I felt, in triangulating other information I've discovered about the family that includes the person who may very well be my father's Chester.

So, I asked. And he remembered: He remembered – vividly, he said – being back in his hometown in eastern North Carolina and riding in a parade to celebrate the first peacetime Armistice Day since 1941. When I searched his local newspaper, I quickly found a news item, in the November 8 edition of the *Washington Daily News*, reporting that "Ensign Ford S. Worthy, Jr. arrived in the city yesterday to spend a 14-day leave with his parents." That blurb, in the section of the newspaper devoted to the comings and goings of regular folks in town, answered my question: When, exactly, had Dad's encounter with Chester taken place? This item in his hometown newspaper seemed to confirm that it was either November 6 or November 7, 1945.

But remember – this particular story is a story within a story. My pursuit of Chester had now taken me to Washington, North Carolina – the original Washington, as my grandmother liked to call it, because it was the first town named for Gen. George Washington, in 1776. Dad has not lived there for 70 years, but Little Washington, as it is also known, shaped him and is never out of mind. It was a small town in 1945 (pop: 9,000) and is not much bigger now. As a child visiting my grandparents there, it was a place where everyone seemed to be related and everyone seemed to know about everyone else's business. When Dad told me he remembered being in Washington for the Armistice Day parade, I knew I would be able to verify that detail. And as I combed through the local newspaper, via an online database, I half expected to come across the first telling of the story about Chester Park. Surely my father had told someone that story!

The parade took place three months after the long, grueling war ended with the announcement that Japan had surrendered. The occasion of the parade would be the "first opportunity," wrote the newspaper editor, "that the city has had to give anything like a welcome to the returning veterans of World War II." The editor added: "The whole county should turn out and pay respect to the boys who have done such a noble job." On Monday, November 12 (since the customary date for celebrating Armistice Day, November 11, fell on a Sunday that year), thousands lined the streets of Little Washington to welcome home hundreds of veterans and servicemen.

My father remembered the details: the route from the high school down Main Street, the marching bands, the convertible he rode in with his friends Harry Walker and Gray Hodges, the three of them sitting on the boot cover in their military uniforms. As Dad recalled the celebratory scene, one that played out that day all across America in small towns like his, midsized cities like Omaha, and larger cities like San Francisco, I realized that this memory had become permanently encoded in his DNA.

There was one other detail he remembered. And here's where this story merges, in an unexpected way, with my and my sisters' stories. You see, another thing my father recalls about that parade on Armistice Day 1945 is that, years later, our mother had told him it was on that day, as he passed by in that parade, resplendent in his full dress Navy uniform, that she first spotted him. She had celebrated her 15th birthday just two days before. He had turned 21 just seven weeks before, on an oil tanker anchored in Tokyo Bay, waiting for orders to return home. Nine years later they got married. She was thinking about him that day, but he was not yet thinking about her. She had not yet become part of his story. Knowing my father, he was probably still wondering what had become of the young boy he had dropped off a few days earlier in Omaha.

I still can't answer that question for sure, but in the next chapter I'm going to delve into the U.S. Census records for 1940 and 1950, and tell you why those and other records point pretty strongly towards one particular boy named Chester.

6

ENUMERATORS AND HEADS OF HOUSEHOLDS

Posted on August 5, 2024

I considered beginning this installment with this cryptic teaser: "Taylor Swift has now entered the story," but instead, here's what I've got:

The 1940 Census included 45 people with the first or middle name Chester, who were born in Nebraska between 1933 and 1937. So says Ancestry. A search for Chesters born in California during that five-year period returned an additional 221 hits. In Chapter 4, I described the reasons for using those parameters in my attempt to find out what happened to a young boy named Chester who was entrusted to my father in the San Francisco airport for a flight to Omaha, Nebraska in November 1945. I won't recap the storyline any further here, other than to remind you that my father will turn 100 in just seven weeks, and for the past 79 years he has wondered what became of that boy. My mission – as a birthday gift to him —is to find out.

By the time I populated the key search fields that produced the above results – Gender, First Name, Birth Year, Birthplace – I had done an exhaustive search for "Chester Park," the name remembered by my father, and I had also investigated scores of Chesters whose last names included "ar" or "ark" or "or" or even "au". To name just a few, there was Chester Harper, Chester Hart, Chester Marsh, Chester Arson, Chester Carson, Chester Clark, Chester Spau, Chester Mark, Chester Short and Chester Sautter.

None of them worked out.

After all that fruitless work, I pivoted, on a hunch that maybe my father was only half right in remembering the young boy's name. I began focusing on *Chesters*, rather than *Chester Parks*. Among other strategies, I did a scan of all the Chesters born in Nebraska, beginning with the nine who were born in 1933; then I turned to 1934. I intended to evaluate each age cohort through 1937. I was screening for the age and marital status of the boy's mother, and I was also looking for some connection to California, while also keeping my eye out for a connection to Omaha, the city where my father had promised to deliver Chester to his grandmother after the flight from San Francisco.

My plan was to carefully vet each and every one of these Chesters, beginning with the 45 born in Nebraska, and then I would repeat the same process with the group born in California.

The first Chester who popped up, from the group born in Nebraska in 1933, was immediately ruled out because his mother would have been outside the age range I assumed, 25 to 35, in 1945. And that was how it went for many of the Chesters I examined. With a quick, cursory review focusing on the mother's age, I was able to dismiss them from further consideration.

The other known detail – the marital status of Chester's mother – deserved to be treated a bit less definitively. I knew from a letter written by my father a month after their airport meeting that Chester's

mother had described herself as divorced. What I've learned in study-
ing the accuracy of census records is that the stigma of divorce,
especially 80-some years ago, sometimes resulted in divorced women
being listed as "widowed" and sometimes even as "married." With that
in mind, I looked for other reasons to rule out a prospect whenever
the mother (or apparent mother) of a Chester was shown as "married"
on a census sheet but without any apparent father listed as part of the
same household. Likewise, when a prospective Chester's mother was
shown as "widowed," I dug more deeply until I could eliminate him on
other grounds.

Why have I used the word "apparent" – in describing Chester's
mother? It's because of what the census can – and cannot – tell us
about the relationships among the people we live with. The census
is constructed around the concept of "households" – a term of art
that means the place where people live and sleep most of the time. A
"household" consists of all the people who live together in a house,
apartment, single room, or other housing unit. In 1940, the reference
person for each household, the person, that is, with respect to whom
all other household members were described, was called the "Head"
of the household. Back then, if a man lived in a household, he was
presumed to be the head of the household. Each member of each
household was described based on their relationship to the head of
the household. Only if Chester's mother was listed as the head of her
household could we know for sure that Chester was in fact her son. If,
on the other hand, someone else was listed as the head of a household
that included Chester, it's frequently not possible to say definitively
how he was related to any other person living in that household.

Consider, by way of illustration, a hypothetical household

composed of a 28-year-old man named Daniel Murray, identified as the head of the household; a 27-year-old woman named Kay Murray, identified as Daniel's wife; and a 6-year-old named Chester Murray, identified as Daniel's son. You might reasonably infer that Kay is Chester's mother – and she probably is, but she could instead be his stepmother, or his aunt, or even, if you're into multigenerational family dramas, a much older half sister; or she might not be legally or biologically kin to him at all. What I learned about interpreting census data is that you need to be careful before jumping to conclusions.

When I pressed the search key to view the 1934 cohort, a list of 13 Chesters appeared on my computer screen. The first name on the list was Chester Sautter, of Scotia, Nebraska, whose presumed mother, Edna, appeared alone in the Parents column of the Ancestry summary. (A slightly modified search in that same census returned another(?) 6-year-old Chester Sautter, in a household that included a second Edna Sautter, who in this listing was described as the wife of Henry Sautter, who was described as the father of Chester – which makes my point about using care when sorting through census data. Were these the same two families, captured separately in two different places, as seemed likely to me, or were these two different families who happened to have the same names?

On the census sheet itself, the first of these Ednas was listed as "married," and a special code indicated she was married but her spouse was not present. Might that circumstance be a prelude to a different marital status five years later, I wondered? But Edna was too old. She (like the second Edna) was listed as 46, and by 1945 both of these Ednas would have been 51 – unlikely, I thought, to have been mistaken by my father for a 30-year-old.

One other Chester on this list also caught my eye: like Chester Sautter, this Chester appeared to be living in a household with just one parent. On the actual census sheet, the census enumerator that day, Anna K. Friedman, had dutifully recorded the following information: This Chester's household was located at 1109 S. 35th Avenue, in Omaha; it was headed by a 59-year-old

widow who had immigrated from Germany, married, and become a U.S. citizen. Her name was Anna Impey. Anna's household was made up of her 27-year-old daughter; her 7-year-old grandson; her grandson Chester, age 6; and a houseman, age 44. The marital status of Anna's daughter, the presumed mother of the two young boys, was designated with a bold "D," for "Divorced."

Two questions included for the first time on the 1940 Census made me feel confident that the mother of this particular Chester was indeed divorced. First, the household member who answered the enumerator's questions that day was identified by an "X", and in this case was Chester's grandmother, who certainly would have known the status of her daughter's marriage. Second, the census taker recorded where each household member had lived five years earlier; all five members of Anna's household were shown as having lived in the "same place" on April 1, 1935 – an indication, perhaps, that this Chester's parents had been apart for some time.

A connection to California came into view as soon as I checked the next census, taken 10 years later, in 1950. By then the household to which this same Chester belonged had moved more than 1,600 miles to the west, to Oakland, California. This Chester, now 15, and his older brother (16) were listed as sons of the head of this household, a 38-year-old man who was born in Nebraska. Also listed was the 38-year-old wife of Chester's father; and, except for some slight age discrepancies between the two censuses, she was clearly the same woman who, in the 1940 Census, was listed as the daughter of Chester's maternal grandmother, Anna Impey. In other words, Anna's daughter was Chester's mother. She, too, like her husband and Chester and his older brother, had been born in Nebraska. Two younger boys, both born in California, completed this Oakland, California, household.

So far, this family seemed like a promising lead. I had (1) identified a boy named Chester, who in November 1945 would have been 11 years old – within a year of the age of the boy my father remembered; (2) I had confirmed the age of Chester's mother; she would have been 33 or 34 in 1945, on the outer edge of the 10-year age range I had assumed, based on my father's memory of a woman who looked to be around 30 when he encountered her; (3) I had established that, in 1940 at least, this same Chester's grandmother lived with her daughter and two grandsons in Omaha, exactly where the maternal grandmother of my father's Chester may have lived when, five years later, Dad delivered Chester to her at the local airport; and (4) I had determined the marital status of Chester's mother at two distinct points in time: in 1940 she was listed as "divorced," and in 1950, she was listed as "married." And moreover, because everyone in this family shared the same last name, it seemed perfectly reasonable to infer, or at least speculate, that this Chester's mother and father were divorced from each other as of 1940 and that by 1950 had remarried one another.

The 1940 and 1950 Censuses, the 16th and 17th censuses taken in our nation's history, offered a detailed framework for understanding this American family – and most all other "households" that existed in those years in the United States. It's a framework full of rabbit holes and dead ends and ambiguities and flat-out mistakes, but it also turns out to be a pretty good starting point for finding my father's Chester.

What matters for my search, of course, is not the state of affairs in 1940 or 1950, but 1945. My next step is to zoom in to see what I can learn about this particular Chester and his family – as of approximately November 6 or 7, 1945. Were his parents still divorced when his mother entrusted him to my father for that flight on that day? Did his grandmother live in Omaha (or at least somewhere nearby) at that time? Did his mother work for United Airlines, a possibility concealed, perhaps, between the lines of the letter my father subsequently wrote (but never sent) to the fiancée of his shipmate? These are just a few of the questions I'm trying to answer.

And in case you're wondering, is Taylor Swift really going to become part of this story. (Answer: I think so, but I can't prove it – not yet.)

7

CIRCUMSTANTIAL EVIDENCE

Posted on August 13, 2024

My father has a well-deserved reputation as a master storyteller. Although I had never heard his story about Chester until two months ago, I've now heard him retell it quite a few times since then – always with relish. He is enjoying the search for Chester almost as much as I am.

Three days ago Dad was retelling the story in a call with the son of a former shipmate. It was that shipmate's fiancée, an airline employee at the time, who set the story in motion when she promised my father, in November 1945, to help him get on a flight out of San Francisco for a brief home leave from Navy duty right after the end of World War II. In Dad's words:

> *"I was supposed to deliver the boy to his grandparents in Omaha. And I got there with Chester and found no one waiting for him. And the airport thinned out – this was 11:30 at night – just me and Chester. I was having all of these thoughts about what was I going to do with*

Chester – one of which included me taking Chester home and asking my mother to raise him. Anyway, about 2 a.m. the grandparents showed up. I didn't have much conversation because the plane I was going on was leaving. So I handed Chester over to his grandparents and took off, and I never heard from him again."

My birthday gift to my father is to find out what happened to that young boy. I have just 40 days left, until September 22, when Dad will celebrate his 100th birthday.

I have introduced you in previous chapters to a family – a "household," in the parlance of the U.S. Census Bureau – that in 1940 lived in Nebraska and in 1950 lived in California. A boy named Chester, 5 years old (though incorrectly listed on the census sheet as 6) and then 15 in these two bookend years, is a part of this household; other clues to whether he is indeed the boy I'm looking for are also leading me in the same direction. My gut tells me this family is a promising possibility, but while I have learned a lot, I do not know nearly enough to say I've found him. Far from it. So, at least for now, I'm keeping certain details, including the family's last name, to myself.

What I know about this family, up to now, I know mostly from the decennial surveys taken of all American households in 1940 and 1950. The Census Bureau releases the kind of personal data I've been examining 72 years after each census is taken. Known as the "72-Year Rule," this means that the next batch of personal details from a census won't be released until 2032, when the 1960 Census will become fully available. These massive compendiums have enabled me to create a map for this particular family. But right now it's an incomplete map; it's more like a roadmap without any roads. The map is dotted with all kinds of data points, but it has no streets or highways – no connective tissue.

The goal now is to fill in enough of the roads to see if the Chester in this family might have intersected with my father on one specific day, either Tuesday, November 6, or Wednesday, November 7, 1945.

When you know who you're searching for, the task of tracking them down is not nearly as difficult as it might seem. Even if you're looking for someone in 1945. That's because of profound advances in the digitization and searchability of the records that document our

Around 1942, Chester's mother moved from Omaha, Nebraska, to the northern edge of Berkeley, California (the uppermost white circle on this map), less than 10 miles from his father's home in Oakland (lower circle). The Golden Gate Bridge – connecting the northern tip of San Francisco to Marin County – had opened just five years earlier. (United States Geological Survey)

lives, from birth and death records, to marriage certificates, Selective Service registration cards, military service records, ship logs, passenger lists, voter registration files, court records, professional licensing records, city directories, and newspapers and magazines. The rapid emergence of AI – artificial intelligence – has further enhanced our ability to search through old, once-analog records with increasing speed and precision.

I've employed all these tools to home in on this Chester and his family. A few examples:

This Chester's mother, who lived in Omaha with her mother and two sons at 1109 South 35th Avenue in 1940, still lived there in 1941, according to the Omaha City Directory from that year. Though not always perfectly accurate, city directories, which list businesses and individuals and their accompanying addresses and phone numbers, can be invaluable for locating people at different points in time. By 1942, Chester's mother had moved to California, where she resided at 960 Stannage Avenue in Albany, on the northern edge of Berkeley, where she was registered to vote as a Democrat, according to Alameda County Voter Registration records. Two years later she was still at that same address. Assuming she had been true to her political party since reaching the legal voting age in 1932 (when she turned 21), she may have voted that fall, for the fourth time, to elect FDR to an unprecedented fourth term as president.

Meanwhile, this Chester's father appears to have lived in San Francisco in April 1940. I learned that from his father's obituary, which ran in the April 26, 1940 edition of the *Omaha Evening World-Herald*. (Despite hours upon hours of looking, I still haven't located this Chester's father in the 1940 Census.) On October 16, 1940, Chester's father registered with the Selective Service with an address in Oakland, signing a draft card listing his race, height, weight, eye color, hair color and complexion. A native of Omaha, Chester's father returned home to visit his mother for Christmas in 1941. By 1942, voter records show that he was registered to vote, as a Republican, at a new address in the Cleveland Heights neighborhood in Oakland. By December 9, 1943, that same draft card, in a cursive scribble on the right margin, indicated that he had moved a few blocks away to 588 Haddon Road, where he stayed put for a while. We know that the entire family – father, mother, Chester and his older brother, and two younger brothers – was living together on Haddon Road when the next census was taken in April 1950.

Those voter rolls, as with many of the underlying records, don't conclusively prove anything more than that a person by the same name of Chester's mother, or father, had registered to vote at a particular address. Each of us is unique, but our names are more often not as unique as we might think. When I was a magazine reporter in Chicago in the mid-1980s, I once dialed a wrong number that was answered by a man who identified himself, *before* I had identified myself, as Ford Worthy – my own, not-as-unique-as-I-had-always-assumed, name.

Proof – evidence you can trust – often doesn't rest well on a single name found in a single place. The satisfying moments in a genealogical hunt like this come when you find that second or third or fourth independent record that breathes confirmation into the first.

There are other discoveries – circumstantial evidence, you might say – that merely lend weight to the theory of the case. You'll remember that Chester's mother told my father, when they met at the airport in late 1945, that she was divorced. So, I was especially intrigued to discover that her address in 1944, on Stannage Avenue on the northern edge of Alameda County, was less than 10 miles from the handsome house in Oakland where Chester's father lived from 1943 until at least 1950.

Circumstantial evidence can sometimes make you wonder whether you've got it all wrong. I had a brief sinking spell when I returned to a data dot that had appeared early on on the roadmap I was building. In a listing of recent births in the area, the April 18, 1944, edition of *The Oakland Post Enquirer* published this item: "To the wife of" – here the name of Chester's father appears – "588 Haddon Road, Oakland, April 1st, a son." The California Birth Index confirmed this baby's full name, complete with the middle name Impey, which, in case you've forgotten, was Chester's mother's maiden name. The new baby was clearly a younger brother for my Chester. Maybe their parents were not so divorced after all, in which case maybe they were not the parents of my father's Chester.

I decided to press on, to turn a potential deal killer into a step forward. Being divorced and having a child together are certainly not mutually exclusive. More important, there was now no doubt about where this Chester's mother was in April 1944: She was unquestionably in Oakland.

When I told my wife about the new baby, who would have been just a year and a half old when his mother put his brother Chester on a plane with my father, her first question was: "Who do you suppose was taking care of the mother's toddler when she and Chester went to the airport?"

I consulted several online sources and quickly learned that Chester's uncle, his mother's brother (Charles Impey), had moved to

California after graduating in 1938 with a medical degree from the University of Nebraska; when his sister took her son Chester to the airport, Charles was working as a doctor at Saint Francis Hospital in the Nob Hill neighborhood of San Francisco. He later moved across the bay to Alameda County, the same county where Chester – and his mother, and his father – lived at the time of the airport episode.

In pulling on this particular thread, I also discovered other nearby Impey family connections. Several of Chester's mother's cousins lived in or around Oakland – which is also where Anna Impey, Chester's maternal grandmother, ultimately wound up herself; by 1948 she had left Omaha and was living with her son's family in Hayward, just south of Oakland. The whole family, it seemed, had abandoned Nebraska for California. To answer my wife's question: There were quite a few family members in the area who might have been available to take care of Chester's younger brother.

My next discovery brought me even closer to the intersection where my father's life may have crossed paths with the very Chester whose family I've been talking about.

On November 13, 1945, just six or seven days after my father's airport encounter with Chester and his mother, a brief item in the society column of The *Omaha Evening World-Herald* reported that Chester's paternal grandmother had returned to Omaha after a seven-week visit in Oakland with her son, Chester's father; her daughter-in-law, Chester's mother; and her grandsons. The newspaper mangled the boys' names, but after checking it against other information, there is no doubt that the report was referring to Chester and his two brothers.

Finding this short item – 33 words long – felt like a major victory. For one thing, I had spent upwards of 20 hours, spread over several weeks, searching, tediously, for something like it in the *Evening World-Herald*, which was the last U.S. newspaper to publish both a morning and afternoon edition on a daily basis. When I came across this item, I was actually looking for news of Chester's trip – the trip from his home near Oakland in the company of my father – to visit his grandmother in Omaha. That was just the kind of society chatter that newspapers from that era loved to share with their readers.

When my name-based searches produced no such results, I kept searching, using other key words; eventually, I searched for the simple word "visit" in the daily editions published during the first half of November, when I knew my father's trip to Omaha had taken place. With the serendipitous discovery of this item, my long, laborious effort was finally rewarded in an unexpected way. Assuming the newspaper's account was accurate and that the item ran soon after Chester's grandmother was back in Omaha, this seemed to further establish the whereabouts of my Chester and my Chester's mother during the relevant window: November 6 or 7.

Ah, but all this is circumstantial evidence, and the circumstances highlighted by this one-sentence news item raised more questions. What does the timing of Chester's grandmother's trip, in such close proximity to that of Chester's trip with my father, tell us? Does it weigh in favor of some emergency that prompted the need to send Chester to Omaha – an emergency, perhaps, that required his mother to head to the hospital after dropping him off? And what, if anything, can we deduce from this trip about the status of Chester's parents' relationship? Anyone reading the newspaper blurb would have assumed from it that the grandmother's visit had been a visit with the entire family, but if Chester's mother and father were living together, why did his mother bother to tell my father she was divorced? Was she looking for sympathy from him?

And finally, remember all those Impeys who had transplanted themselves to California? One of them – Frank Impey, Chester's mother's uncle – shows up on an Ancestry record titled the "Haywood/Barnhart/Impey/Park Family Tree." Now, in case you missed that — as I did myself several times — here's the name of that family tree again: the "Haywood/Barnhart/Impey/*Park* Family Tree." The Park branch included Grace Edith Merrill Park, Frank's wife and, by marriage, Chester's great-aunt. When I first noticed the name Park, my imagination kicked into overdrive. Could this well-constructed family tree be a sign that the name Park is, in fact, a part of this story?

There is still lots to puzzle over.

8

A FAVOR FOR A FRIEND,
OR A PATRIOTIC THANK-YOU?

Posted on August 27, 2024

There is one potentially crucial clue to this story that, until now, I have parried. I have mentioned it, I have alluded to it, and in one weak moment I even partly relied upon it.

But now, with just 26 days to go before my father turns 100, I have less than a month to wrap up my birthday gift to him: to find out what became of the young boy he encountered at the San Francisco airport in the first week of November 1945, in the immediate afterglow of the end of World War II.

And to do this, I have to deal head on with an inference that *could* be made from a letter I discovered in Dad's files shortly after he first told me the story about Chester. In Chapter 2 I mentioned this letter, which Dad wrote in early December when he was temporarily stationed at a Navy base in Norfolk, before he returned to San Francisco and a new ship. The date is important because it establishes that the airport episode recounted in the letter was still fresh in his mind.

He wrote the letter to thank Sarah Liggett, his shipmate's fiancée, for her help in getting him a flight out of San Francisco for a brief home leave to eastern North Carolina. I don't know exactly what Sarah did to help my father, but she worked for one of the airlines and when he showed up at the airport and stopped by the United Airlines check-in counter, without any ticket or even any idea of what flight he might take, the staff seemed to have been primed to lend him a hand. As he wrote to Sarah later: "They said that they had already been notified about me from the downtown office."

One airline employee in particular – Dad refers to her in his letter as the "baggage lady" – seems to have gone out of her way to help him get a seat. She counsels Dad to be patient. He waits – for several hours. Finally, a seat on a flight to Chicago opens up, and he boards the plane for what would be the first leg of a cross country trip to eastern North Carolina. Just as the engines are warming up, the baggage lady comes onto the plane and tells him that his bag hasn't made it; she asks him to deplane and find his bag. He gets off the plane, looking "high and low" for his bag, before he and the baggage lady conclude that it was probably put on an earlier flight to Chicago.

Today – 79 years later – Dad can look back at this mundane moment and recognize it as a pivotal juncture. At the time, though, in the late afternoon on an early November day at the San Francisco airport in 1945, all my father knew was that his bag was heading somewhere – to Chicago, perhaps, but in any case without him – while he still had no idea when or even if he would be able to find his way to North Carolina to see his parents and girlfriend for the first time in nearly a year.

In his letter to Sarah Liggett, Dad described what happened next. Referring to the baggage lady, he wrote:

"So she got me on the 5:30 plane. When she put me on she asked if I would do a favor for a friend of hers & an employee of United Airlines. I said sure so she introduced me to a lady about 30 who told me she was going to the hospital & she was divorced & had to send her little son to visit her mother in Omaha"

The letter stops there, abruptly. Curiously, it was never sent – I know that because I found it in Dad's files, in an unstamped envelope, never sealed. But it nevertheless contains clues that have propelled my search for the boy named Chester. To wit: Clue No. 1 is that the boy's mother was "about 30" years old. Clue No. 2: She was divorced. Clue No. 3: She had to send her son to visit her mother in Omaha. I've dissected each of these clues in previous chapters.

What other clues or possible suggestions does this densely packed excerpt reveal?

It tells us the departure time of my father's flight – which, after factoring in the speed of commercial airliners then, plus a brief stopover along the way, is consistent with Dad's recollection that they arrived in Omaha at 11:30 that night.

It tells us that the person assisting my father – the "baggage lady," as he described her elsewhere in the letter – was the person who introduced him to Chester's mother, after asking him if he would do a favor for a friend of hers who worked for United Airlines.

We also know from the letter that Dad spoke directly with Chester's mother. Folks who know my father will recognize that as an important clue in and of itself. He would have almost surely asked her all kinds of questions – and if he had finished that letter (the letter that stops all of a sudden, in mid-sentence), I know he would have told Sarah much more. In fact, knowing his propensity for writing down good stories, he and I are continuing to look through his files in search of a fuller account of what actually happened at the San Francisco airport.

The clues I've just described, while useful, have never struck me as dispositive. But a separate question, one so hidden in the ambiguity of my father's letter that I passed over it repeatedly for a long time, could be a case closer – or not.

Was Chester's mother an airline employee?

Put a different way, does the scene in this act require five actors, as I initially assumed?

The baggage lady.

The baggage lady's friend, who is an employee of United Airlines.

Chester's mother.

Chester.

And my father?

Or, are there only four players in this scene?

In other words, was the baggage lady's friend also Chester's mother? Are they one and the same person?

Who is the baggage lady referring to when she speaks of asking my father to "do a favor for a friend of hers & an employee of United Airlines"?

Why is this such a potentially pivotal question? If I conclude that Chester's mother worked for United Airlines, that would add a new variable to the equation I'm trying to solve for, in addition to the boy's name, the boy's age, the mother's age, the mother's marital status, and the place of the grandmother's residence. Adding this new variable would enable me to rule out any Chester I find whose mother did not work for United – even if that Chester otherwise checked all those other boxes. But if I find a Chester who checks all the boxes – every single one, including a new requirement that his mother was employed by United Airlines – that would be like picking up a specific grain of sand from among all the beaches in the entire world. That's how ChatGPT sized it up for me after I added this new condition to the criteria I had given it earlier.

I've struggled with how to analyze this question.

I've approached it on two parallel tracks.

First, I contacted Sarah Liggett Reed's oldest son to ask whether his mother (who died 14 years ago) may have kept old letters or diaries. It was a long shot, but maybe she was a well-organized pack rat like my father. Dad and I had a delightful hour-long telephone call with Skip Reed, who's now in his 70s, but he had no light to shed on my dilemma.

Second, I sought out input from people who interpret language for a living. I've reached out to lawyers, detectives, journalists, forensic investigators, and linguists. Everyone agrees that the baggage lady's friend was an employee of United Airlines. But there is no consensus on whether that same person – the baggage lady's friend who worked for United – was Chester's mother.

A linguistics professor who teaches syntax and phonology reasoned that the phrasing used by my father in his letter to Sarah suggests that a single favor was involved, and that favor, he speculated, was to help a young boy get to Omaha. As he observed: "If there

Brian Hsu, a linguistics professor at the University of North Carolina at Chapel Hill, helped me better understand what may have happened at the San Francisco airport by analyzing the structure of a crucial sentence in my father's letter to Sarah Liggett. (Photo by Ford S. Worthy)

had been two separate people who needed favors, I would probably expect this to have been described as two separate favors instead of one." A second linguistics scholar told me he thought Dad's choice of words was "awkward" but not "ill-formed" – "just ambiguous." He added: "To understand the 'friend of hers,' 'employee of United Airlines,' and 'lady about 30' (i.e., the boy's mother) as co-referential (i.e., referring to the same person) would be a reasonable inference."

Parsing those conjoined noun phrases helped frame the possibilities, but it could only take me so far. What I was really wrestling with, as one of the linguistics experts gently pointed out, was something deeper: trying to understand what was actually happening between my father, Chester's mother, and the baggage lady. The words and syntax in Dad's letter mattered – but the surrounding context mattered more. Here was a national airline allowing a mother to send her young boy on a long, nighttime flight, with at least one stopover on the way, to a city in the middle of the country – at a time when commercial air travel was still a luxury, and when children, especially, rarely flew even with their families.

My surface-level dig into 1940s-era airline policies around "unaccompanied minors" turned up no real standardization. Where rules existed, they seem to have been informal and situational compared with today's elaborate requirements. Examining the history of air travel by unaccompanied minors, while definitely thought-provoking, couldn't in the end rule out my father's understanding of what transpired at the San Francisco airport.

There are at least two theories – in addition to my father's simpler explanation – that might fit with the context we have to work with.

If Chester's mother did, in fact, work for United Airlines, as one journalist speculated, perhaps she brought Chester to the airport intending to place him in the care of the flight crew bound for Omaha. When she saw my handsome father in his Navy uniform and was assured by the ticket desk that he was an okay guy, she agreed to let Dad chaperone her son – all the while knowing that her employer, United, would actually be in charge of Chester.

That possibility does fit neatly with another detail: the boy's remarkable familiarity with ailerons and other parts of a plane's anatomy – knowledge that might well have come from growing up around a mother who worked for a company whose business was flying airplanes. But then again, if Chester's mother was so comfortable handing over her child to my father because her United colleagues would be watching out for him, wouldn't someone with United have met them at the Omaha airport? What my father recalls is this: When their plane touched down just before midnight, the terminal quickly emptied – and he and Chester were entirely on their own.

Another theory – one I find promising – hinges on the hospital reference in Dad's letter to Sarah. According to my father, Chester's mother told him, during their brief exchange, that she was "going to the hospital." We don't know why she said that, or why she felt the need to say anything at all. But if she was facing an emergency – something urgent enough to warrant a trip to the hospital – might that explain why United made an exception to whatever policy it normally followed for unaccompanied minors?

These are reasonable inferences and interpretations, and I cannot flat out tell you they are wrong.

In the next chapter I'm going to tell you what I believe – and why.

9

"THAT SOUNDS EXACTLY LIKE SOMETHING MY GRANDMOTHER WOULD HAVE DONE."

Posted on August 27, 2024
(originally as part of the prior chapter)

My father has always had an exceptional memory – especially the type that neuroscientists call "episodic" memory, which is defined by the authors of a book called *Psychology* as "the collection of past personal experiences that occurred at particular times and places." My father's "semantic" memory – the kind that experts describe as the "network of associated facts and concepts that make up our general knowledge of the world" – is pretty good, too. But at 99 years and 11 months, Dad's ability to accurately recall particular experiences that he has lived through is off the charts. I'm biased, but I think he may be a "superager," a term for a tiny slice of the elderly population whose memory is equal to or better than people 30 years younger. I have always felt this, but in recent years I've come to know it based on working with him on various projects that involve remembering.

A year ago he and I collaborated on a small book called *Memories of My Father*. It was a memoir about his own father, who was born in 1881 and died in 1956. (By the way, you can find it in the North Carolina Collection at Wilson Library on UNC's campus in Chapel Hill.) Among my responsibilities for that project was to fact check the stories Dad told about his father. Because my father's father was active in many spheres of life in eastern North Carolina, and because my father's mother was a prolific writer who filed away her letters, speeches, diaries, calendars, travel itineraries, and the like, I was frequently able to confirm my father's memories against original source material.

As he and I were working on the memoir, Dad recalled the moment he heard the news that Japan had accepted the Potsdam Declaration, the first signal that World War II was about to end. He was sitting in the wardroom on the *USS Lackawanna*, playing poker with Dudley Reed (Sarah Liggett's future husband) and two other fellow officers. When the radio blared out the news, Dad remembered having a 4 in the hole, a 2 and a 3 and an ace up. He told me he remembered hearing the news bulletin and then drawing another ace to win the pot. The last poker game of World War II, he called it.

It was a good story, and maybe the essence of it was true, I thought, but then later while perusing his files, I came across a memo he had written that very day, August 10, 1945, documenting each small moment, from the "vile" toast he had had for breakfast to the B-29s he had observed flying towards Japan from his ship's position between Saipan and Iwo Jima. His memory of the poker game that day, including the extra quarter he wagered after hearing the news, was virtually a carbon copy of his contemporaneous, written summary of the same day. Maybe he recalled the poker game so well because he had recorded the details, in writing. Maybe his special aptitude for remembering is due to his penchant for writing down his observations and experiences. Whatever the reason, his memory is extraordinary.

The story of Chester is seared into my father's episodic memory. Not every detail, of course. But the heart of what he experienced – what he remembers *feeling* as he spoke with Chester's mother – was surely unforgettable. I know him well, and I know when I can trust his memory. What he remembers – and what I trust – is a young mother giving up her seat as a gesture of appreciation for a young Navy officer, who, along with more than 16 million Americans, had helped defend her country during World War II. She was not simply handing over her child out of necessity because she needed a responsible adult to accompany her boy on a flight to Omaha. Something more was at work: As my father remembers, she was honoring him for his service.

My interpretation of the airport scene is, admittedly, open for debate. But after spending hours upon hours imagining what might have happened, here's how I've reconstructed it:

At a nearby ticket counter, the baggage lady's friend – I'll call her Mary – is helping a customer. That customer is Chester's mother. Mary learns that Chester's mother is trying to find someone who can accompany her son to Omaha – perhaps so she can attend to an urgent matter at a hospital. Mary alerts her friend, the baggage lady, that there may be a mother willing to give up her seat – if only a trustworthy chaperone for her son can be found. The baggage lady, who has been dealing with my father for the past hour or so, trying to get him on the next flight, knows just the person. She tells my father there may be a seat on the 5:30 to Omaha – if he's willing to accompany a young boy to meet his grandmother at the airport there. When Dad agrees, she introduces him to Chester's mother.

Ford S. Worthy, Jr. (at far left) with his *USS Lackawanna* shipmates: Bob Cratty, Dudley Reed, whose fiancée Sarah Liggett helped FSW Jr. get a flight out of San Francisco, Bill Edwards and T.C. Wicker (left to right). Reed, Edwards and Bill Spain (not pictured) lost the "last poker game of World War II" to FSW Jr., on August 10, 1945. (undated photo, ca. 1945)

Chester's mother, deeply grateful, thanks my father profusely – first for his Navy service, then for his willingness to look after her son. She explains that an emergency has come up, and she needs to get to the hospital to deal with it. My father, always quick to connect with people, then and now, would have responded with warm thanks of his own and a flurry of questions – a friendly interrogation aimed at finding common ground with a stranger. My inquisitive father would have wanted to know where her husband and other relatives had served during the war; maybe that's how he learned she was divorced.

Before they parted, he would have told her not to worry about Chester. He'd see to it that Chester got safely to his grandmother. And just as he and Chester turned to board the plane, Chester's mother, filled with gratitude, may well have called out to my father: "Thank you again – for your service."

The number of ways this scene might actually have played out is infinite.

I'm still convinced that, deep in my father's files, I'm going to find a letter or a memo or a note that clears away some of the mystery about what really happened. Even if Dad can't remember writing it down, I believe he did – because he wrote everything down.

In the meantime, I'm the playwright here.

And in my script – until I unearth more evidence – logic is not necessarily going to have the final, absolute word. In my script, Chester's mother was *not* an employee of United Airlines.

And that just happens to be a convenient conclusion, because I know now, after weeks on one particular trail and beyond any reasonable doubt, that the mother of the Chester who I have come to believe is my father's Chester was not an employee of United Airlines, nor was she an employee of any other company, for that matter. To use the description she gave of herself two years earlier when registering to vote, she was a "housewife."

The mother of my Chester grew up in a prominent family of physicians in Omaha and married into another affluent Omaha family with interests at various times in real estate, steel, and meatpacking. Both sides of Chester's family – his mother's parents and his father's parents – lived near Hanscom Park in the historic Midtown neighborhood of Omaha, within walking distance of the exclusive Field Club, a storied country club that catered to the city's elite. Chester's mother was well taken care of. She may never have worked for anyone.

Would she have given up her seat to a young sailor, by way of honoring him and all the brave soldiers who had fought for her and her country, while also thanking him for watching over her young son on a flight from San Francisco to Omaha? In my first conversation with a member of this Chester's extended family, his niece, an Episcopal priest in Knoxville, Tennessee, told me: "That sounds exactly like something my grandmother would have done."

10

CHESTER'S BACKSTORY

Posted on September 8, 2024

To understand what became of Chester, the young boy whose mother placed him in the hands of my 21-year-old father, a Navy officer back on U.S. soil for the first time since the end of World War II, I first should tell you where Chester came from.

If you're just joining this story it will be helpful to know a few things that I've established over the course of 13 weeks of searching for Chester as a gift to my father, who will celebrate his 100th birthday two weeks from now.

On approximately November 6, 1945, two weeks after my father's return from the Pacific, where he had served as an ensign on an oil tanker, he was allowed a short home leave. My father was homesick to get back to eastern North Carolina to see his parents and his girl-friend, so much so that he decided to fly commercial rather than travel for free via the Naval Air Transport Service.

The golden age of air travel was just beginning to boom, but it was super-expensive. A study commissioned several years ago by an air-line industry group estimated that in 1941 a typical flight from Los

Angeles to Boston was worth $4,439 in today's dollars; at the time, that would have been the equivalent of well over a month's salary for a junior Navy officer like my father. Flying on a commercial airline meant you were most likely either a business traveler or had plenty of money.

At the San Francisco airport, an airline employee introduced Dad to a young woman who gave up her seat to him as a patriotic gesture of appreciation. She also asked my father – a stranger to her, though one decked out in his full dress Navy uniform – to be responsible for delivering her son Chester to her mother, who would be waiting, she assured him, when the flight arrived in Omaha. Chester, 11 years old and impressively knowledgeable about airplanes, began calling my father "Daddy" soon after they took off. You can try to poke holes in this story, but my father is a "superager," and he swears by his memory of how it all played out, and that's what I'm going with, too!

So where did Chester come from? What was his backstory? Much of what I've learned about him and his family is from public records; more recently I've been able to confirm certain details with members of his family, several of whom I've been in touch with; and finally, some of what I'm going to tell you is speculation on my part and could be wrong.

I could fill a small book with what I know about Chester and his family. His roots ran deep in the Midwest. His mother, Dorothy Helen Impey, was born in Omaha in 1911 and grew up in the city's affluent Midtown neighborhood. Dorothy's father, Chester Impey, was a third-generation physician; her mother, Anna Dittrich Impey, was a nurse with an eighth-grade education who had immigrated from Germany. A few blocks to the east of their home was a 15-room mansion

built by banking and freight mag-
nate Charles Henry King; King's
grandson, future president Gerald
Ford, lived there for a few weeks
after his birth in 1913. Just blocks
to the south was the exclusive Field
Club, a country club that catered
to the elite of Omaha. The Impeys
were almost certainly members of
the club, judging from news items in
the local newspapers.

Chester's father, Douglas M. Pratt,
rose rapidly through the U.S. transportation industry to become president of a New York Stock Exchange
company that accelerated the shift
from streetcars to buses in cities
throughout the country during the
1940s and 1950s. (undated photo,
courtesy of Nancy Pratt Ellis)

From newspapers and other
public records, it's easy to see that
Chester's mother lived a privileged
youth. Her social calendar as a teenager included hosting tea dances at
the Field Club, where at one she led the grand march. After finishing
at Central High School, she toured Europe for two full months with
her mother and other Omahans, visiting London, Brussels, Wies-
baden, Baden-Baden, Lucerne, and Interlachen, before *flying* – which
was a unique experience back then for most people – from Geneva
to Paris and then returning home via the *Empress Australia* in August
1929, just before the stock market peaked. Unlike the vast majority of
women at that time, whose education never went beyond high school,
Dorothy continued with her schooling. She seems to have spent four
years at a Catholic college in Omaha before graduating in 1933 from
Creighton University, where she was a member of the Choral Club
and the basketball team. She stood out further among her female

classmates by the degree she earned: a bachelor's in philosophy, in contrast to the kinds of programs women more typically pursued at the time – teaching, nursing, and social work.

Before she got her degree, she got married – to Douglas McLain Pratt, a fellow Omaha native born just a few months before Dorothy in 1911. I don't know whether they knew each other growing up, but their families lived just a mile apart, and they went to the same high school. The Pratts, like the Impeys, were almost surely members of the Field Club, where Douglas' mother was a regular for bridge. Douglas' father, Clayton A. Pratt, had been valedictorian of his engineering class at Stevens Institute of Technology. He worked for an engineering firm in Omaha before marrying Evelyn Fitchett, described in a newspaper account as one of the city's "fairest daughters."

Clayton pursued a wide variety of business interests. He was chief engineer for Armour & Co., the giant meatpacking company. He and his wife were involved – though to what extent I don't know – with a company called Omaha Structural Steel Works, now a division of a private company that is still in business; they were two of its four incorporators in 1906, and Clayton was described in an advertisement a year later as the "Manager" of the company. The company was highly successful for many years, providing steel for the Nebraska State Capitol building in Lincoln, steel castings for steam locomotives, and, during World War II, artillery shells and landing craft tanks. Clayton also helped form Omaha Heavy Hardware in 1908, and a few years later he played an executive role in establishing a manufacturer of incinerators and garbage machines. Perhaps most consequentially, he was an active real estate investor; the county registry of deeds is peppered with transactions in his name. Clayton and Evelyn also invested in property in Sonoma County, California, among other places.

The elder Pratts kept an active social calendar in Omaha, and they also travelled widely: New York, Northern California, Los Angeles, San Diego, Excelsior Springs, Missouri, a winter-long stay (with Douglas, when he was 7) in Wilmington, North Carolina, and frequent, lengthy trips to Colorado, where they had a second (or maybe it was a third or fourth) home. All these destinations, along with the family's acquisitions of art and collections of antiques, were documented in the local newspaper of record: the *Omaha World-Herald*. In June 1931, the *World-Herald* reported that Douglas and his mother had recently returned to Omaha from a yearlong stay in Denver.

BRIDE FETED POSTNUPTIALLY

MRS. DOUGLAS M'LAIN PRATT

Chester's mother, Dorothy Impey Pratt, several months after her marriage to Douglas McLain Pratt. (the *Omaha Morning Bee-News*, September 22, 1932)

Within a year of that particular sojourn, Douglas and Dorothy were married and living at his parents' home while Dorothy finished her bachelor's degree. The *World-Herald's* competitor, the *Omaha Morning Bee-News*, added to the couple's origin story by featuring a photo of an elegant Dorothy, noting that her friends had feted her "post nuptially" – "her marriage having come as a surprise." A year after marrying, Douglas and Dorothy had their first child, Charles.

The following year, they had Chester.

Chester Allen Pratt, the co-star of this story, was born in Omaha on May 15, 1934, to Douglas and Dorothy Pratt.

At some point around this time, Dorothy and Douglas divorced. Family members are not sure exactly when, but one of their grand-daughters told me they remained divorced for about 10 years, which seems about right considering the evidence I've excavated so far. The census records document their status in 1940 as "divorced" and in 1950 as "married." Based on Dorothy's father's obituary, they were probably not living together in late 1938. An earlier data point – a newspaper account in April 1935 – could relate to the timing of their divorce. According to the *Petaluma Argus-Courier*, Douglas, then 23, was jailed for drunk driving after an accident near Healdsburg, California, where he had recently purchased a ranch. Maybe his drinking figured in the divorce. Or was it a gambling problem, as another family member suggested. Or maybe it was something else? Or maybe they just weren't meant for one another.

Except … it seems, they were meant for each other.

Douglas was busy with a burgeoning career in the transportation industry. According to *Running the Rails*, a book about the history of Philadelphia's public transit system published in 2016, he started out as a clerk in Omaha after graduating from the University of Nebraska and then moved to Oakland to become the general manager of Pacific City Lines, which was rapidly buying up streetcar systems on the West Coast. He registered for the draft in 1940 but appears to have remained a civilian throughout the war. Another of his granddaughters told me that during this period he was constantly travelling up and down California and was said to have always been able to obtain rationed goods that were in short supply on account of the war.

Chester's parents, Douglas and Dorothy Pratt, on their farm in Pennsylvania. (undated photo, courtesy of The Rev. Dorothy Pratt)

Around 1942, Dorothy moved from Nebraska to California with their two sons. She lived on the northern side of Berkeley – roughly seven miles from Douglas' house in Oakland. A granddaughter of Dorothy and Douglas told me: "It was never clear during this period whether they were divorced or merely separated. There weren't a lot of stories told in our family. But they were definitely an 'item,'" she said. In 1944, Douglas and Dorothy had their third child, a son, who would have been a toddler when Dorothy met my father at the airport. And later, sometime after the encounter between Dorothy, Chester, and my father, she and Douglas apparently remarried and had a fourth son.

By the time Douglas and Dorothy officially got back together, Douglas, still in his 30s, was already a director of Pacific City Lines. Based on the important leadership roles he played at PCL and its parent company, National City Lines, it seems fair to say that he influenced the transformation of the American urban transportation industry as it shifted rapidly from electric-powered streetcars to cars and buses. In 1952 he moved his family to Baltimore to run the bus company there, and a few years later he took the top position at Philadelphia Transportation Company, where he oversaw a period of price increases, declining ridership, and a tumultuous relationship with union transit workers. The author of *Running the Rails* wrote that Douglas Pratt was a hard-driving, imperious executive who expected his colleagues to address him as "Mr. Pratt". Mr. Pratt eventually rose to the very top of the industry, becoming president of Chicago-based National City Lines, a New York Stock Exchange company that owned or controlled dozens of urban transportation systems, including bus companies in Los Angeles, Tampa, St. Louis, Tulsa, Houston, and Montgomery, Alabama, where in 1955 Rosa Parks refused to give up her seat to a white passenger on a bus operated by Montgomery City Lines, a subsidiary of National City Lines.

This, then, is where Chester Pratt came from.

In the next, penultimate, chapter of this story, I plan to tell you what became of Chester Pratt.

Dr. Chester C. Impey, Chester Pratt's grandfather, with Chester's older brother Chuck
(at left) and Chester. (ca. 1936-37, courtesy
of The Rev. Dorothy Pratt)

Chester Allen Pratt (May 15, 1934-March 6,
2009). The search for a boy named Chester
was set in motion by the memory of an
airport encounter in November 1945, when
Chester was 11 and FSW Jr. was 21. (undated photo, Ancestry)

11

CHESTER, FOUND!

Posted on September 16, 2024

In my dreams, the NBC anchor Lester Holt is wrapping up his *Nightly News* broadcast. "We leave you this evening," he intones, "with a heartwarming story from Omaha – where a 100-year-old Navy veteran of World War II is reuniting with the young boy he took care of in a most unlikely encounter 79 years ago today."

Lester then turns to a huge video wall of my father shaking hands with 90-year-old Chester Allen Pratt, the two of them standing in the concourse of present-day Eppley Airfield in Omaha, surrounded by me and my sisters, and Chester's brothers and children, and our extended families, a United Airlines ticket counter visible in the background.

"Chester, I've been wondering how you turned out for a long time," my father says. "Tell me, how was your flight to Omaha this time?"

Chester Pratt died 15 years ago, on March 6, 2009, at age 74.

After he crossed paths with my father, Chester grew up in Oakland, graduated from high school, tried college for a year or two, and then served as a quartermaster in the Navy for several years before following his father's imposing footsteps into the transportation industry.

The record of his life is out there – as it is for each of us in different ways – but the part of it that has become visible to me over the past three months is relatively sparse, especially compared with the well-documented business career of his domineering father. Like all of us, Chester Pratt lived a life that was both ordinary and extraordinary. It would be presumptuous to try to distinguish the ordinary moments of his life from the extraordinary, because only he, and perhaps those closest to him, could do that. But I'll tell you what I've learned about him.

He and his first wife Betty were both 20 when they married in 1954. They had three children. Betty died young at 50 in 1983, and their middle child, Clay, died in 2003 after a brief illness. I was not aware of these sorrows when I first reached out to their oldest child, Doug Pratt, in July, as I was first beginning to wonder if Chester Pratt might in fact be my father's Chester. Doug also told me that a rare disease he has lived with for years had added to the parental worries that his father carried with him. Chester married Neva, his second wife, in 1984.

Along the way, Doug told me, Chester worked for bus companies in Tampa and Philadelphia – doors no doubt opened by Chester's father, Douglas Pratt, who by 1955 headed the Philadelphia Transportation Company and later became the president of National City Lines, a New York Stock Exchange company that controlled dozens of urban transportation systems throughout the United States. Chester later went into the truck leasing business, a niece recalls. He and his young family lived for a number of years in Pennsylvania, where they were able to regularly visit his parents' farm in the Gettysburg area.

He eventually moved to Texas, forming a company that specialized in using sprayed concrete to construct and repair swimming pools. Doug told me his father capped off his many-faceted business career as a developer of residential real estate. Chester partnered with a friend of his father to develop hundreds of acres between Denver and Colorado Springs. Doug believes Chester and his brothers inherited this property from their parents. All I've found in the public record about it is a trail of regulatory applications to secure water rights. Sadly, Chester's brother Chuck, who was just a year older and might best have been able to confirm some of this chronology, passed away in 2023.

In his final years Chester can be found quoted and pictured in the pages of *The Kerrville Daily Times*, restocking a Christian food pantry operated by a group of churches in Kerr County, Texas, where he lived with Neva until his death in 2009.

Chester's son Doug told me his father was captivated by World War II. When Doug was a kid, his father, a voracious reader, consumed books about the war at the rate of one or two every week. Like his father, Doug also served in the Navy, focusing on explosive ordnance disposal. After his own military career ended, Doug remembers a business trip to Texas where he and his partners visited his father. Chester, brimming with enthusiasm, took Doug and his partners on a tour of the National Museum of the Pacific War in nearby Fredericksburg, about 25 miles from his father's home in Kerr County. Doug's partners were amazed by Chester's gift for revealing the smallest, most interesting details as he guided them through each gallery in the museum. "My dad was a great storyteller," Doug told me.

The museum opened in 1967, in part as a tribute to Fleet Admiral Chester W. Nimitz, who grew up in Fredericksburg and became one of the foremost naval strategists of his time. I have taken a virtual tour of the museum, and among its many displays is one that shows visitors how oil tankers like my father's performed the critical job of refueling other naval vessels while underway at sea, so they could continue in hot pursuit of enemy warships. Pioneered by Adm. Nimitz, this innovation allowed American aircraft carriers and their escorts to operate for extended periods in the Pacific, far away from the bases they were previously tethered to by their insatiable need for fuel. The fleet oilers were a decisive advantage for America in overcoming Japan – and a source of pride for my father.

Seeing the refueling-at-sea exhibit reminded me of one strand of this story that I've not been able to pin down. It's about Charles Impey, Chester's uncle on his mother's side. Charles Impey became a doctor, like his father, grandfather, and great-grandfather. And like his sister, Chester's mother, he too moved from Omaha to the Oakland area. And like my father, he served in the wartime Navy. One document I came across suggests that Chester's uncle served on a ship that participated in the invasion of Okinawa, the largest amphibious assault during the entire Pacific campaign; it lasted 82 days in the spring of 1945, resulting in 50,000 Allied casualties and 100,000 Japanese casualties, and included hundreds of kamikaze attacks from the air. My father was there, too, for that monumental battle.

As I moved my cursor through the virtual tour of Adm. Nimitz's museum, I wondered if maybe, just maybe, my father might have intersected with Chester's uncle as their two ships maneuvered alongside each other during a refueling operation in the Pacific – even before Dad met Chester and his mother in San Francisco later that same year.

As these stories converged in my imagination, I was transported back to that flight to Omaha 79 years ago. As overwhelmed as my own father was by the responsibility of looking after young Chester, it was also true that for their six or seven hours together Dad had had a captive audience: an 11-year-old boy, sharp as a tack, whose knowledge about airplanes was astounding.

My father would have begun their conversation by telling Chester Pratt about his namesake, of a sort, Adm. Chester W. Nimitz. Dad can't remember what they actually talked about, but he must have regaled Chester about his experiences, still so fresh in his mind, aboard the USS *Lackawanna* – the story about refueling the destroyer escort

Taken from an unidentified Navy ship, this photo shows the *USS Lackawanna* (AO-40) (at right, against the horizon) refueling the *USS Wisconsin* (BB-64) in the Pacific Ocean approximately 600 miles southeast of Tokyo. During this operation, the *Lackawanna*, an oil tanker, transferred 14,285 barrels of fuel oil to the *Wisconsin*, a battleship. It hung in my father's bedroom for many years. (August 18, 1945)

commanded by the son of President Roosevelt on April 12, 1945, the very day FDR died, during the earliest phase of the Battle of Oki-nawa; the story about the typhoon, on June 5, that produced 100-foot waves and wreaked such terror and havoc that the ship's commander, paralyzed with fear, was later relieved of duty; the story of seeing dozens of B-29 Superfortresses headed northward, on August 10, to unleash some of the last bombs dropped on Japan in the last days of the war. And wouldn't my storytelling father, a master raconteur just like Chester himself became, have told the young boy what it had been like to sail into Tokyo Bay on September 10, just eight days after Adm. Nimitz had signed the Japanese Instrument of Surrender on behalf of the United States in a ceremony on the quarterdeck of the battleship *Missouri?*

And finally, as a sweetener on top of these war stories, my father, who always appreciated a good coincidence, would have told his new friend about a connection to another Chester: Chester County, South Carolina, a place shaped in his imagination by the idyllic memories passed down from his mother, whose forebears had lived there for generations.

My sisters and I have heard all these stories – and so many more.

The young boy who would have heard my father's stories, as they flew to Omaha 79 years ago, sitting side by side, maintained his fasci-nation with airplanes and aviation throughout the rest of his life. In the Navy he was a quartermaster, a specialist in mapping and charts and navigation systems. His older brother Chuck served in the Air Force as a jet engine mechanic. His younger brother Clay was a corporate pilot. Clay's son is a chief pilot, a position that typically is responsi-ble for managing teams of pilots and supervising their training and safety compliance. One of Chuck's daughters recalled that for years Uncle Buster, as the family knew Chester, and his brothers attended the annual Oshkosh airshow, a gathering of aviation enthusiasts that is among the largest in the world.

Chester's son Doug also became a pilot, after completing his own long career in the Navy.

When I set out on this journey to give my father a special gift for his 100th birthday, I had no idea how it would pan out. I was searching for a person named Chester Park, and I wound up finding someone named Chester Pratt. There are other discrepancies and inconsistencies that have intruded along the way, each of which I've acknowledged – and then refuted or explained as well as I could. But in the end, the person I landed on – an 11-year-old boy named Chester; whose mother was 34 and divorced; whose grandmother lived in Omaha, Nebraska – checks too many of the boxes to be a coincidence.

By my calculation, the probability when I began that any single person would check all the right boxes was less than one out of 140 million, the approximate population of the United States in 1945. ChatGPT, assessing the same odds, told me that my quest was like picking up a specific grain of sand from an entire beach – a probability, it reckoned, of around 0.00000073%.

While the numbers are plenty validating, it's the connection to flying that makes me so certain I have found the right Chester. What really convinces me that my Chester, Chester Pratt, and my father's Chester, Chester Park, are one and the same is the boy's lifelong passion for airplanes. At age 11, Chester was so shockingly knowledgeable about planes that he could describe how those hinged surfaces on the trailing edge of an aircraft's wings – ailerons, as he knew to call them

– added to the stability and maneuverability of an airplane.

A critique of my search for Chester could fairly argue that I was looking for what I found: that a certain bias, in where I looked and what I looked for, tilted my search towards finding a young boy of a certain age; whose mother, of a certain age, was divorced; and whose grandmother lived in Omaha, Nebraska.

But in the end, I found what was impossible to search for in digital databases and other impersonal records. I found someone whose early attachment to airplanes was not simply a youthful infatuation but a genuine passion that coursed through his entire life. I found someone whose family has flying in their blood; someone who, in his weekly calls with his own son, a licensed pilot, insisted on hearing about the nuances of every flight Doug took. "Every time I flew," Doug told me, "Dad wanted to hear about everything."

"My dad," Doug said, "he knew a lot about airplanes."

And now – I've returned to my dream … that dream from the very beginning of this next to the last chapter of my birthday gift to my father.

Maybe it's a dream, but could it be real? Lester Holt is sitting with my father in Doug Pratt's living room in South Carolina. In his hands, Doug is holding a treasured possession bequeathed to him by his father, a scale model of an F/A 18, an aircraft commissioned decades ago by the Navy. Nearby is a statue of a Navy airman that Chester had kept in his office – and left to Doug.

In my dream, I am asking myself, why would Lester Holt or anyone else want to share this story – share it with the whole world – this story about the precocious little boy and the young Navy officer, now days from turning 100, who delivered the boy safely to the boy's grandmother in Omaha?

And then before I can answer, I see Lester in my dream, speaking to my father, and to me and my sisters and our children, and to Chester's children and their children, and to all of you, too. Lester is looking straight into the camera, signing off: "Please take care of yourself, and each other."

12

HAPPY HUNDREDTH, DAD!

Posted on September 22, 2024
My father's 100th birthday

This birthday gift to my father, this story I have been telling for the past three months, grew out of my father's story about a mother who honored him for his wartime service and then entrusted him with her young son for a flight from San Francisco to Omaha. As stories often do, my father's story inspired other stories, and this story will no doubt spawn still other stories – and remind us of old stories.

One of my favorites came recently from a friend from high school, someone I hadn't heard from in decades, who posted a comment about her own father when he was stationed with the U.S. Army in Korea. His unit took in a local boy, sheltering and befriending him, and coming to love him. When eventually it was time for her father's unit to return home, he and his fellow soldiers cried when they had to leave the boy behind. "Dad talked about him for the rest of his life," she wrote me, "wondering what had happened to him."

Doug Pratt, Chester's son, emailed me a few weeks after we spoke by phone in July. He told me a new story, one that had emerged from and was now fused with a story that I retold in the last chapter. The story I heard first was about the visit Doug had made perhaps 20 years ago with his father to the National Museum of the Pacific War in Fredericksburg, Texas, not far from where his father lived. His father's knowledge about Adm. Nimitz and the museum's comprehensive exhibits exceeded that of any tour guide. His father's enthusiasm for sharing what he knew was infectious.

The new story occurred shortly after our initial phone conversation. Doug wrote me that his grandson Jeremiah was visiting him in Charleston, South Carolina, where Doug lives, and Doug took him to the naval museum there to see the USS *Yorktown*, an aircraft carrier that fought in the Pacific campaign to take the Philippines, Iwo Jima, and Okinawa, among other legendary World War II battles. (In the final stages of the war, my father's oil tanker and the *Yorktown* operated in the same task force – but that's another story.)

Jeremiah is roughly the same age as his great-grandfather Chester was when he met my own father 79 years ago, and he's an avid reader just like Chester was. Doug wrote that "Jeremiah stopped at every interactive display and had to read every page to me, stopping now and then to ask a question or to tell me how cool this or that plane was. He could tell you every plane that was flown off the *Yorktown* during the war."

When it was time to leave and Jeremiah got in the car, he told Doug it had been the best day of his vacation. And when Jeremiah left Charleston to return home, Doug gave his grandson a book which his own father, Chester, had given him about the Battle of Midway, a major naval battle that marked a turning point in World War II. Doug told me that his time with Jeremiah, an experience now melded together with his memories of his father and with this story remembering his father and my father, was a blessing to him.

Stories bind us together. They teach us. They entertain us. They reveal who we are or at least who we want to be. They demonstrate our values – our love for family and country, our empathy for strangers, our desire to form new connections, our concern for equality and justice. Stories help us remember – and the stories that are only partly told or sometimes not told at all, can cause us to forget or to never know – things that are, or should be, important to us.

These are big, weighty words – love, family, selfless service – and I understand that some of you will skirt past them. And that's okay.

But for me, this story, a gift to my father but also a gift from him to me, is more than a summertime amusement. It has been my way of thanking him for all his stories – stories that first shaped him, and then me. And now I am blessed to share his stories – and his storytelling – with my own family, and with you. Thanks, Dad – and Happy 100th!

The Pratt family, including Chester, standing at far left, with his parents Dorothy and Douglas, seated, and Chester's son Doug in her lap. (ca. 1956-57, courtesy of The Rev. Dorothy Pratt)

13

IT WASN'T SUPPOSED TO END LIKE THIS

This story was supposed to have ended on September 22, 2024, exactly one hundred years, to the day, after my father was born on Main Street in Washington, North Carolina. The story was supposed to have ended with the birthday gala my sisters and I threw for him on the very day he turned 100, celebrating with 300 adoring friends and family, spanning generations, who sang clever tributes to him and hung on every word as he regaled them with stories from a lifetime. As his friends arrived for the festivities that day, a pose-worthy 1929 Model A Ford – polished to perfection – greeted them outside Dad's club, and as they departed a few hours later, some would have driven by the marquee on the old Rialto Theatre, which displayed its own greeting, "Happy 100th Birthday Ford."

By design, that was also the day I posted the final installment of my story about my father's story about a young boy named Chester. The next morning the local Raleigh newspaper, *The News & Observer*, ran a front-page article about the search for Chester. And a day or two after that, Dad's smiling face showed up on a jar of Smucker's on the

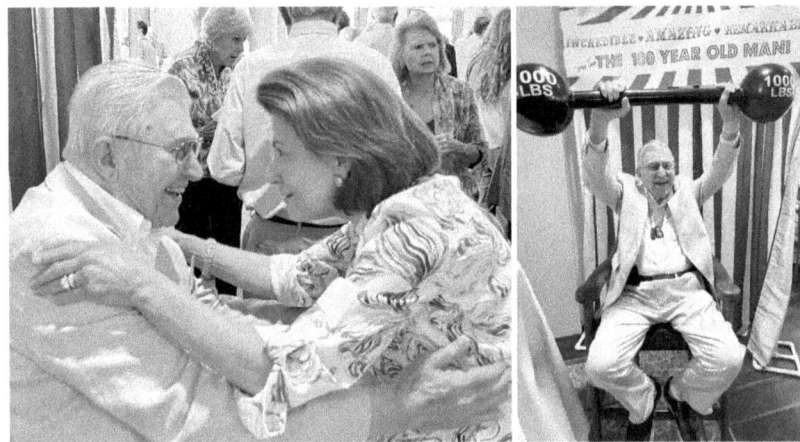

Dad enjoyed being the center of attention at his 100th birthday party. (Photos by Blanche Williamson)

Today show, with Al Roker, the NBC personality, saying, quite accurately: "Ford Worthy's secret to longevity: he can connect with anyone."

And then things returned to normal.

For a while.

———

It's late in the afternoon on a Monday in February, five months after my father's 100th birthday. I am alone in his condo writing this epilogue. If Dad were still here, I'd be walking through his front door right now, as I did about this time every Monday during the last few years of his life. I saw him on other days, of course, but always on Mondays.

I would have called ahead to ask if he thought the local seafood market might have any Spanish mackerel, his favorite; and he would have told me, "Probably not yet."

"It's a little early in the season for buying Spanish mackerel," he would have told me.

It was not unusual for me to arrive to find an empty apartment, which sometimes meant he was out doing errands in his bright yellow Jeep. If he wasn't home when I got there, I could often find him in the small fitness center across the street where, beginning in his mid-80s, he spent precisely 24 minutes every day on the elliptical. He had things to do. He was not someone who enjoyed waiting for you. He had remained active, independent, and full of life to the very end.

Before preparing dinner for the two of us, I would sometimes take him for a drive to see a newly developing part of town. After dinner we would just talk; we both cherished this time together. At 10 or 11 p.m., when it was time for me to head back to my home 30 miles away, I always asked if he needed me to do anything; he expected so little that I looked forward to the chance to do even the smallest things: helping him make his bed, clipping his toenails, troubleshooting his iPhone.

Dad died on November 9 – three days after a hard fall, tumbling backward. He was having dinner at his club, and he got up to go say hello to a friend seated nearby.

On the day he died, two of my sisters were keeping vigil in the ICU at the hospital when a phlebotomist entered the room. He glanced at my sisters, then at my father, greeting them: "My name is Chester, and I've come to take your blood."

My father, by then no longer aware of the world around him, would have delighted in the chance to get to know another Chester.

14

WHAT BECAME OF
THE YOUNG SAILOR?

In my original post on Facebook, as part of the very first entry that launched this story on June 18, 2024, I signed off with this exhortation: "So ... Facebook, do your thing! Help my father find out what became of Chester Park?"

So now, let me tell you what became of my father.

That brief home leave to North Carolina, which began in early November 1945 at the San Francisco airport, was extended until the end of the year. The Navy temporarily assigned my father to the Naval Operating Base in Norfolk, Virginia – close enough to his hometown in eastern North Carolina that he was able to drive home for weekend visits and celebrate Christmas with his family. Before heading back to San Francisco, my father went to a debutante ball in Norfolk and a holiday bash in Washington, North Carolina, the small town where he had grown up. After years of war, normalcy had finally returned.

His return trip to the West Coast, where he was to report for a new assignment aboard a new ship, began on December 30. He set out hitchhiking to Cape Charles, Virginia, and then, in sequence: He bummed a ride to Salisbury, Maryland; and another, to Camden, New Jersey, with a young couple from Florida who made room in their junk-filled car for him; next, he took a taxi to the Philadelphia airport; and then an early-morning train the following day to Washington, D.C. Exhausted, he discovered he might be able to catch a 12 noon Eastern Airlines flight to Atlanta and then continue on to New Orleans, before realizing he could get on an earlier American flight to Chicago. When he landed there, the temperature was 23° F, and the tarmac was covered with ice. Then, another plane to Los Angeles, with stopovers in Kansas City, Wichita, Amarillo, Albuquerque, and Phoenix; and a final leg, by plane, to foggy San Francisco, where he reported to duty on January 2, 1946 – exactly 12 hours and 15 minutes late.

And to his surprise, nobody said a thing to him about not being on time.

Why, you may be asking, am I telling you about this cross country odyssey, when it has nothing to do with the story I'm supposed to be telling you?

Because, in fact, it has everything to do with telling you what became of my father after his life intersected, ever so briefly, with the life of a young boy named Chester. You see, my father wrote it all down. In this case, he described every leg and each false start of his coast-to-coast journey in a numbingly detailed, 14-page letter to his parents. This was his M.O. – and throughout his century-long life, he never stopped writing it all down.

I can tell you, with such authority, what became of my father because he left such a detailed record of his life. His experiences from his youth, playing practical jokes with the neighborhood boys along the banks of the Pamlico River; his life-shaping time in the Navy; his countless business dealings; letters to friends and associates; notes from telephone calls; highlights from his travels; his strategies for boosting the trajectories of his children and grandchildren; the make, model, and year of purchase for every car he had ever owned; his analysis of his medical options; the unsolved problems – "cockleburs," as he called them – that he had not yet conquered; the insights he had accumulated over the years that seemed, to him, to represent wisdom – he wrote it all down. He also filed away what others had written down: letters, certificates, contracts, ID cards, memos, logs, licenses, notices, receipts, ticket stubs, clippings, statements, maps, deeds, titles, itineraries, diplomas, brochures; virtually any piece of paper or record of any kind that passed through his hands – even his dance card from that debutante ball in Norfolk just before Christmas in 1945 – everything was a candidate to be saved and filed, so he could find it quickly when he needed it.

He wrote it all down.

On June 25, 1946, he was honorably discharged from the Navy and he returned to the University of North Carolina at Chapel Hill – hoping, initially, to become a doctor. He graduated a year later with a major in zoology. When med school was not in the cards, he and his brother-in-law started their own grading company.

If he were telling this part of his story, he would pause here to recount the many life lessons he took away from working in a small town with his sister's husband, and those insights would then segue into his formative experiences as an employee of the Hoell Motor Company, the local Ford dealer. In 1954, he married my mother, nine years after she first spotted him in the Armistice Day parade in their hometown right after the end of World War II. She was the best thing that ever

FSW Jr. with two of the greatest loves of his life: Isabel Carter Worthy (my mother) and the Pamlico River. During his life he skippered rowboats, canoes, skiffs, sailboats, and a succession of *Seaworthy*-christened powerboats. (undated photo)

happened to him: a smart, beautiful, supportive partner through 67 loving years of marriage. They began married life by moving from their hometown, Washington, to Charlotte, where he had taken a job in the city mortgage department of The Equitable Life Assurance Society, and within a few years they had started a family (I was the first of four) and he was in the real estate business in Raleigh as right hand man to a brash, savvy mentor who bestowed still more life lessons upon him. Dad eventually went off on his own as a commercial real estate appraiser, broker and developer. A book published in 2021 included him among those who shaped Raleigh in the second half of the 20th century.

That would be one way of summing up what became of Ford S. Worthy, Jr., my father.

It wasn't an accident that in his business life he became a broker: someone who brings people together. He had an uncanny, fearless knack for making connections and cultivating relationships with people of all ages, from all backgrounds.

In his zeal and zest to connect, he came at you in a multitude of ways. He would have been a terrible politician, because he didn't care much about optics or being politically correct. But like a good politician, he made you feel like you counted – and he understood the importance of calling folks by their names.

He had a special talent for bonding with strangers. On a research mission for the Chester story last summer, I dropped him off at a restaurant on Main Street in Washington while I parked the car. By the time I joined him inside, he was seated at a table with a man and woman he apparently had just met while standing in line. After the couple left, he and I were finishing up our lunch when the waitress unexpectedly brought us cake and ice cream, cheerily announcing that there would be no charge; our check, she said, had already been picked up. The woman Dad had met while waiting for a table had given him her business card, so I immediately emailed to thank her for the kind gesture. Here's part of what she wrote back:

"You are so welcome. I've lost a husband to brain cancer in 2009 and we lost my 31 year old after coming out of the army in February to suicide by gunshot. It's been tough, but we try to focus on the positive ... you and your dad totally made our day. My late husband and late son were loving, beautiful, friendly people like your dad. You two be safe in your historic searching."

It was not unusual for my father to strike up conversations with strangers – even if they seemed not in the mood to engage. After he died, my sister Marty recalled a visit to the doctor's office where our father began chatting up a young nurse with whom he probably had little in common. "He asked his usual set of questions," Marty said, "but she wasn't biting. I was rolling my eyes thinking, 'Dad, she doesn't want to talk to you.' And then he asked her, 'Tasha – how long does it take you to get your hair done?' And bingo!" said Marty. "He had hit upon a subject she wanted to talk about. He left the doctor's office with one more friend."

His circle of friends – always wide – didn't shrink as he aged. It's true that by the time he died, very few of his contemporaries were still alive. But the number of people whom he considered friends, and who felt the same about him, was constantly expanding. Like many "people" people, he nurtured his relationships, going far out of his way (sometimes literally) to keep in touch, often dropping by unannounced to pay a quick visit; he kept up his active participation in his church, in a half-dozen social clubs, in neighborhood groups, and with his beloved "Zetes," the college fraternity he pledged in 1942. He was frequently the ringleader in pulling friends in for a late afternoon drink beside the pool at his Raleigh condo or at the "sittum" at his place at the beach. He was the instigator of countless trips, parties, and reunions (including regular reunions with his Navy shipmates).

What was different about Dad was that at times he would almost *push* you into a relationship with him. In his 80s he planted several thousand live oak trees at a farm in Beaufort County, where his childhood roots were. When the trees were a few years old, he began a personal campaign – Johnny Appleseed-like – to convince people to transplant his trees along roadsides, in cemeteries, on the grounds of churches and parks and playgrounds. To him nothing could add more beauty to a streetscape or churchyard than a majestic live oak, with its thick, gnarled branches draped with Spanish moss.

The problem was, to take him up on his offer, you had to be really committed. You had to be willing to dig up a sapling, haul it to a new location, transplant it, and then water it like crazy for at least a couple of years until it could get established. Dad made this his mission, writing letters, arranging meetings, mapping out exactly where a young tree would look nice, and explaining in detail how it should be cared for in order to survive. I remember being with him on one sizzling summer day, standing on the edge of a parking lot with the assistant city manager of Washington and three members of the building and grounds committee of First Presbyterian Church, as he explained why the world would be a much better place if only they would agree to convert several parking places into a place for his live oak trees. He could find something you didn't know you needed and then sell you on it so thoroughly that you ended up thanking him for thinking of you – while becoming a friend in the process. Today his trees are growing all over his hometown.

Of all the ways he connected with people, storytelling was his favorite. With the right story he could reach across life's invisible divides, helping others feel seen and understood. Many years ago my son was going through a rough patch. He was working in the produce department of a grocery store – not where he had expected to be at that point in his life. "Granddaddy" wrote him a carefully crafted letter describing his own "involvement" with fruits and vegetables – 10 of them in all, beginning with the artichokes he stole from a neighbor when he was 5, and ending with the crop of corn he planted in a poorly conceived partnership with his brother-in-law, at age 24. There was a personal moral – a life lesson – associated with each of the plums, pears, sweet potatoes, cucumbers, and so on that he wrote about. For example, his

To my father, no tree was more majestic than the live oak. He grew thousands on his farm in Beaufort County near the Pungo River, and he later made it his mission to persuade local officials to transplant them alongside roads, in cemeteries, and in parks in his hometown of Washington, N.C. His grandsons Hoyt Lewis (center) and Thomas Hester joined him for a major harvesting operation on March 1, 2016. (Photos by Marjorie H. Worthy)

discovery of a wild strawberry patch when he was 6 taught him that the small, knobby fruit he found in the field was often as sweet or even sweeter than the large, glossy, perfectly formed specimens sold in the grocery store.

My father's colorful stories, leavened with nostalgia and often a touch of mischief, drew you in, and by the time he got to the big-picture advice, you were engaged, curious, and perhaps ready to absorb a life lesson. His letter to this grandson continued:

> "[T]hink of yourself as one day owning a produce store … Study the inventory. Learn the names of all the produce that you sell. Sometimes buy a fruit or vegetable, take it home, cook it and eat it. Learn how to pick it out, keep it fresh as long as possible, salvage it."

He concluded the letter with a monetary incentive:

"Take notes each day about your experience. Think of yourself as a spy, a double agent working for the [grocery store] on the one hand and transmitting intelligence reports to me, secret agent FSW Jr., on the other. If you send me a report (no more than one page) by email two times each week telling me what you are doing and what you have learned, I will send you a check amounting to $10 for each secret report."

My son, now 35, spoke movingly about this letter at his grandfather's funeral service late last year: "It was quintessential Granddaddy," he said, "turning a simple job into an opportunity for growth and a lesson in observation, ownership, and lifelong learning." More than 400 people were there to pay their respects – and not one could have doubted that this life lesson had been absorbed.

15

AN ELECTRIC MOMENT

My father was interested in really knowing people. That was how my search for Chester started – Dad had wondered for decades how that boy had turned out.

When Dad first told me the story about Chester, on a Monday night last June, I was incredulous. I found it hard to believe, bordering on shocking, that a young mother would have turned over her child to a total stranger, albeit a Navy officer in his dress blues. But even more unfathomable, how could it be that my father, the most prolific, inventive, engaging storyteller I have ever known, had never told me this improbable story. In all our time together, I had never heard the barest hint of it. When Dad went on to tell me he had occasionally tried to find Chester over the years, scanning phonebooks and city directories when travelling to San Francisco, quietly searching without telling a soul, I immediately promised not only to find Chester but to learn as much as I could about Chester and report back.

At first, Dad didn't take my vow seriously. In fact, for the longest time he was skeptical that I had found the right Chester. More than once he reminded me that the young boy he had accompanied on the flight to Omaha was named Chester *Park*, while my search had ultimately converged on someone named Chester *Pratt*. My father was entertained by my unfolding tale, but he was even more energized by the possibility of connecting with characters in the story who had been true friends.

Take Sarah Liggett Reed and William Dudley Reed. Dad and Dudley Reed had served side by side on the *USS Lackawanna*, an oil tanker that serviced the Pacific fleet during the war. They had been playing poker in the ship's wardroom when the news broke on the radio that Japan would accept the Potsdam Declaration ending World War II. Sarah, Dudley's then-fiancée, was the airline employee who had promised to help Dad find a flight out of San Francisco for the home leave he yearned for. Sarah and Dudley were people with whom my father had had a real relationship.

Midway through the arc of my research, I spent several weeks tracking down Sarah and Dudley's oldest child, Skip Reed, whom my father had never met. We talked with Skip for an hour, by phone. Ostensibly, we were hoping Sarah or Dudley, both of whom were deceased, might have told Skip and his siblings about my father's adventure or, better yet, might have memorialized it in a diary or letter. The truth, though, was that my father wanted to know how his old friends' lives had played out. He was fascinated – and amused – to learn from Skip that Dudley, who had hated the Navy, had wound up re-enlisting a year or so after the war ended. Skip told us his father put in another 13 years as a Navy man before going into business as a chicken farmer after watching a movie called *The Egg and I*. And Dad reciprocated, filling in Skip with a condensed version of his own life.

As the call ended, my father told Skip he was already looking forward to their next call.

As the weeks and chapters progressed – and as it became clear that I was on a trail that just might be leading somewhere – Dad's attachment to the search for Chester steadily grew. He began calling it "our" project, as in truth it had always been. I began to hear through the grapevine that he was regularly updating his friends on how our story was developing.

Our routine went like this: I did my research throughout the week, mostly by sifting through databases and analyzing online sources in the evenings. When I had enough material for a chapter I would write it up. When a new installment was nearly ready, Dad and I would carefully review it during our Monday visits. Sometimes he would scribble his comments on my printed drafts, but he preferred for me to read each new chapter out loud to him. Our editing sessions resulted in frequent corrections and clarifications, and often he was able to add new details. For instance, I read him a passage from Chapter 5 in which he and his friends Harry Walker and Gray Hodges were triumphantly riding down Main Street in the Armistice Day parade after the end of the war, seated together on the back seat of a convertible. At the words, "back seat," Dad abruptly stopped me: It was not a "back seat," he said. "We were sitting on the boot cover."

My father cared about our story.

Our story had begun as a simple search for someone he had met, fleetingly, long ago, but it had now become a shared meditation on memory and connection. Dad was now fully invested.

After dinner, after the table had been cleared of all but his bowl of ice cream, Dad invariably would spread out folders full of memorabilia and papers that he thought might help. His files included the original, typewritten orders from his service in the Navy, the translucent onionskin paper used in that era still holding up after all these years. The files were rich with watch lists, personnel orders, reimbursement records, ship organization binders, book inventories, mail receipts, and programs and correspondence from reunions and trips over the years to see his shipmates. Using copies of the daily deck log for his ship, we plotted exactly where in the Pacific he was in August 1945 – (31° 30' N 136° 30' E) – when he and Dudley Reed and their fellow officers Spain and Edwards played what Dad liked to call "the last poker game of World War II."

As my summer of research stretched into August 2024, I was finally able to verify the date on which Dad's encounter with Chester and his mother had taken place: It was almost certainly November 6, 1945, and there, to prove it, was the order from the Office of Commandant, Twelfth Naval District, granting him permission to depart San Francisco, California, on that day and directing him to report, for temporary duty, to the Fifth Naval District in Norfolk, Virginia, on November 14. A yellowed receipt in his files showed that after he returned to San Francisco, on January 2, he received $257.36 for his travel expenses.

The most electric moment of our collaboration occurred when a small notepad slipped out of a file folder documenting my father's time in the Navy. I knew immediately what it was: an early incarnation of the "portable memory" he carried with him wherever he went. For decades and decades it was his practice to record – in pocket-sized notebooks – detailed information about people and places in his orbit. Names, addresses, phone numbers, (eventually) email addresses, birthdays, and

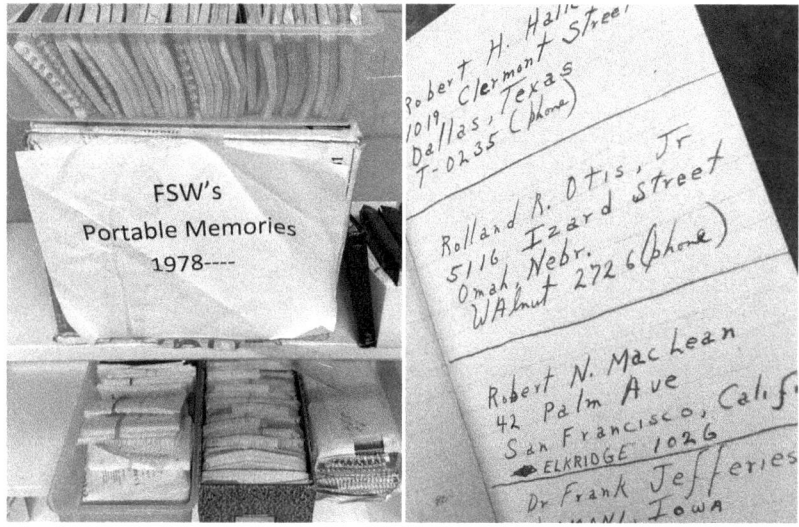

Dad's "portable memories" – those 3 x 5 notepads he always carried in his shirt pocket – helped him maintain and manage his wide network of family, friends, and associates. Pictured here are several dozen dating from the late 1970s. The photo at right is a page from a notepad covering the first half of 1946. When it slipped out of a Navy folder while Dad and I were searching for clues about his encounter with Chester, I felt a jolt of adrenaline – and anticipation.

much, much more, like the names of spouses and children, and when and where he had most recently seen or spoken with them, or how they were connected to him and to others. An entry might list the names of every tenant at a building he owned; the slip numbers at a dock he used for his boat, the *Seaworthy*; references to replacement parts for auto components and household devices. Directions and instructions and reminders – these, too, he frequently recorded in a portable memory. Until he fully transitioned to the iPhone, I cannot remember ever being with him when he was without his portable memory. He used these portable memories to supplement his own formidable memory, regularly consulting and updating them. In the age of the iPhone, this might not seem so unusual; in 1945, it was anything but ordinary.

One thing I know about my father: When Dorothy Pratt placed him in charge of her 11-year-old son Chester, he *wrote down the details*. He would have written down Dorothy's full name, along with her address and phone number in the Bay Area. He would have written down her mother's name and address and phone number in Omaha. He almost certainly would have asked her for, and written down, the name of a relative or friend of Dorothy's in San Francisco *and* Omaha, in case the handover in Omaha didn't go as planned. My father would have written down the details – most likely, in his portable memory. And he would have kept the portable memory that contained that information, just as he kept the dozens of small notepads that I found after he died, organized chronologically in a box in his closet.

When the small portable memory fell out of the Navy file folder, landing at my feet, I felt a jolt of adrenaline. Up to this point, I had searched most of his files, looking for some record, some trace, of who my father's Chester really was. Up to this point, I had found only a brief acknowledgement of the airport episode in a letter written by Dad – the letter that furnished the key clues that had guided my search. All this time, my father and I had been searching, again and again, through file folders, letters and notepads, looking for more clues – but I had never seen this particular portable memory.

The notepad was 3 ½" by 5 ½" and contained eight pages of names, addresses and a few phone numbers before morphing into a diary or ship's log covering 22 days in the spring of 1946. There were only 30 people listed, not nearly as many as I had expected, but here, in this portable memory, I was sure I was about to find a clue that would confirm I was headed in the right direction or, perhaps, point me in an entirely new direction. Either way, I knew the clue that was about to surface would be a game-changer.

I raced through the notepad – looking for a name (Chester or Park or Pratt or Dorothy) or an address (in Omaha or San Francisco or Nebraska or California) or a date (November 6 or 7 or 8) in 1945.

I turned back to the first page for a second run-through, this time slowly tracing my finger over each entry. And this time, I recognized an oddly abbreviated form of something I was looking for: "Omah" followed by a comma, and then "Nebr" followed by a period.

The full entry, in my father's familiar handwriting, was:

> *Rolland R. Otis, Jr.*
> *5116 Izard Street*

And then the next line with the odd abbreviations that stood for Omaha, Nebraska.

And finally, *"WA lnut 2276"* – the style for telephone exchanges from that period, meaning 9-2-2-2-7-6.

With help from Google I immediately placed this address and this telephone exchange in the heart of Walnut Hill in North Omaha, about three miles away from the neighborhood where *my* Chester was born and had spent his early childhood, where both of Chester's parents had grown up, and where his grandparents were prominent members of the community.

Was Rolland R. Otis, Jr. the missing link that would finally connect the Chester of my father's memory to the Chester of my summerlong search?

No, my father told me, matter of factly.

This man, Rolland R. Otis, Jr., and most of the other names in the notepad, Dad told me, were from Dad's brief stint with the *USS Ajax*, a repair ship that my father was assigned to after returning to the West

Months after completing the story of my search for Chester, I stumbled across this photograph of my father speaking to his *Lackawanna* shipmates at their reunion in 1993, held in Omaha, Nebraska. The reunion newsletter in which it appeared included this tantalizing caption: "Ford Worthy telling of his first visit to Omaha." (August 1993)

Coast from his home leave in North Carolina.

And what about the daily log in the same notepad? That turned out to be the record of my father's final weeks in the Navy, aboard the *USS Norton Sound*, which picked him up in Honolulu and carried him back across the Pacific, through the Panama Canal, bending around Haiti and then wending homeward past Florida and North Carolina to Norfolk, where he was released from active duty in late June. This final voyage took place from April 28 to May 19 – and he wrote it all down. Had he not been discharged – and had he remained with the *Ajax* – he would have been an eyewitness to the first peacetime atmospheric nuclear weapons tests conducted a few months later only 15 nautical miles from the *Ajax's* position near Bikini Atoll in the Marshall Islands.

In the months since he died, I have painstakingly gone through his papers. My sister Marty discovered a letter, undated and apparently hand-delivered, from Sarah Liggett Reed to Dad, instructing him to call a fellow United Airlines employee, Miss Marco Christensen, "after 9:00 o'clock A.M. tomorrow." This letter seems to have been sent to him just before his home leave, for Sarah's colleague was "working eastbound control" for United and "will do all possible to get you out." She, like Sarah and Dudley, died years ago; but that long-ago job was important enough to make it into one record of her life. According to her obituary, Marco Christensen Callister gave up her teaching job when World War II started and moved from Salt Lake City to San Francisco to work for United Airlines.

I've found only two other fragments that testify to my father's story about Chester. Chester Parks with an "s" appears, alongside Sarah Reed, on a list Dad made of out-of-state trips and important events that occurred between 1935 and 1953; and while thumbing through a Navy newsletter, I stumbled across a photograph of Dad, microphone in hand, speaking to his *Lackawanna* shipmates at their reunion in 1993. That reunion was held in Omaha, and the caption below the photo is a tantalizing echo of Chester. It reads: "Ford Worthy telling of his first visit to Omaha." So, maybe he had told his story before.

Whatever else my father may have written down – whatever he may have written down about his encounter 79 years ago – because I am just about certain he did – I believe whatever he may have written down is still hidden – tucked away in an envelope or buried in a folder I have yet to find.

Or maybe it has been lost?

Or perhaps the record of his encounter with Chester is one detail he never wrote down.

16

FILE NO. H-266

I posted the final installment of the original story on September 22, 2024, the day of my father's 100th birthday. At the outset of this project, back in mid-June, it had never crossed my mind that I would still be posting updates as summer turned into fall. Instead, it seemed likely the story would peter out after two or maybe three installments. To my surprise, though, and to my father's utter delight, the story kept gaining momentum. And I could sense that he was proud of it.

The day after his birthday party was a Monday. That evening I read him a long article that had appeared that morning on the front page of *The News & Observer*, the local newspaper. The newspaper story was a story about our story, and it was illustrated with a picture of Dad as a 21-year-old Navy ensign and a second photo of him at age 99.

Now, months later, I am truly coming to the end.

If the main story was about the search to learn what became of a young boy named Chester, these final chapters have been about what

I reviewed thousands of documents for this story, including these from my father's extensive files. As I was writing the final chapter several months after he died, I came across a manila folder I had never seen before, labeled "H-266 Chester Search." In it was a clipping of the newspaper story about our search for Chester. It was published the day after his 100th birthday, and after I finished reading it to him that evening, he gave me his final verdict on our own story.

became of a young sailor named Ford S. Worthy, Jr.

I am back in my father's condo on a quiet afternoon – a Tuesday in February. After my father's funeral service, someone told me they were fighting back the urge to feel sad; they were resisting, because sadness was not an emotion they wanted to associate with his memory. Sitting at a table in his dining room, I look around now and fight back that same, natural ache.

Instead, I will myself to see the reminders all around me as happy memories. Colorful placards from his birthday party are propped against one wall. The table where months earlier the two of us shared our Monday dinners is now stacked with family photos. A half-full bottle of his favorite wine, scuppernong, sits on a nearby counter. Three magnifying glasses are at rest on his desk. Waiting to be claimed, like everything else here, his Carolina blue blazer is hanging in his closet.

Deep in this same walk-in closet is an array of massive file cabinets, still to be gone through by me and my sisters before we sell Dad's place. I pull open several drawers, marveling at the sheer mass of paper within. The files are meticulously organized – he was the son of a librarian and the husband of a librarian. At the very rear of the bottom drawer of one of these file cabinets is a manila folder I've never noticed before. It is File No. H-266 and is labeled "Chester Search."

Inside this folder is a draft of several of the early chapters of our story and a clipping of the newspaper piece published the day after he turned 100. I remember reading that article to him that same evening. The moment is etched in my mind. It is as fresh today as if it happened yesterday. My memory of that moment is another of his many gifts to me. After I finished reading the article to him, he smiled and gave me his final verdict: "I never bothered to tell you the story," he said, "because it never seemed to be that interesting. But you took a good story and made it into a great story."

Ford S. Worthy, Jr. surrounded by his "FAM" on the day he turned 100, September 22, 2024. That Carolina blue blazer he liked to wear for festive occasions now hangs in my closet. (Photo by Blanche Williamson)

Acknowledgements

The story about my search for a boy named Chester first appeared as a series of Facebook posts in the summer of 2024.

I realized, shortly after the first post, that while Facebook was an ideal starting point, it was lacking in other ways. It was a good place to connect with amateur genealogists and Internet sleuths who could be helpful in sifting through the universe of possible Chesters. But if I wanted to share the story with my father's many friends, as I did, without shortchanging the rich narrative I felt it deserved, Facebook was less than ideal. Many of his friends, and mine, are not "on" Facebook. And even if they were, Facebook, while great for sharing photos and pithy comments, is not made for lengthy, essay-ish pieces like the "chapters" that came to comprise this story. I'm sure online readers who made it to the end were worn out from all the scrolling. Still, I started on Facebook, and I finished on Facebook.

After Dad died, the original story, which had seemed so complete with the final post on his 100th birthday, suddenly felt unfinished, so I wrote four new chapters as a sort of extended epilogue. While working on the final section, I was unable to resist the temptation to tinker with how I had told certain parts of the original story. My subsequent editing efforts were made mostly at the margins of the story – straightening out awkward syntax here, choosing a better word here and there. But I did make two substantive alterations: I remade the part of the story in which I considered whether Chester's mother was an employee of United Airlines, dividing it into two separate chapters – Chapter 8, devoted to how experts analyzed that question, and Chapter 9, explaining my own theory. I also added some new material to Chapter 7 about the Impey family, including an observation based on a family tree that I somehow overlooked in my earlier haste to keep the story moving. In fact, if I could have a do-over of any single moment in this project, I would spend more time looking into whether there is a connection between the name my father always remembered for young Chester – Chester *Park* – and the same surname that appears as part of his lineage through his grandfather Impey's brother, Frank, who married a Park.

To make the story accessible beyond Facebook, I later decided to have some copies printed up the old-fashioned way. The final written version eventually led to an audio recording of the story – an audiobook – which provides another means for people to enjoy this birthday gift for my father.

I first realized this was more than just a detective tale when the daughter of one of the earliest Chester Parks to appear on my radar screen wrote me a poignant note about her father. Linda Yazdani and I had both believed, for a moment, that her father might be my father's Chester. After we both concluded otherwise, she wrote to me: "It's a wonderful story and our family has enjoyed the possibility that our father could have been involved." She continued: "With the advancement of technology, storytelling is becoming a lost art. It is so important to share memories and humorous stories with our children and grandchildren as it is something lost in genealogy searches. I do believe our fathers could have had a long friendship had their paths crossed."

I found Linda via LinkedIn, which, like Facebook and Ancestry, was an indispensable tool for tracking down and communicating with people as I pursued this story. To Linda I was a complete stranger asking for information about her father and an event that took place before she was born. Not only was she willing to engage with me, but she went out of her way later to thank me and to encourage me to keep searching for the real Chester. "How blessed your family is," she wrote me, "cherish the time you have." She also invited me to come meet her family in Southern California. Hers was not the only reaction like this.

Father and son enjoying an oyster on the half shell during Thanksgiving 2021. (Photo by Steve Mattox)

I did a lot of research for this project, and, in particular, I want to credit a few books I read and enjoyed, and which informed certain segments of the story: *Democracy's Data: The Hidden Stories in the U.S. Census and How to Read Them*, by Dan Bouk, a detailed account of the 1940 Census; *Psychology*, an introductory psychology textbook by Daniel Schacter, Daniel Gilbert and Matthew Nock, which I dipped into to better understand how scientists think about certain types of memories; and *Running the Rails: Capital and Labor in the Philadelphia Transit Industry,* by James Wolfinger, who devotes a full chapter to National City Lines and Douglas M. Pratt, Chester's father.

I also want to thank the many folks on Facebook, including people with whom I had no prior relationship, who contributed ideas or information that helped me home in on Chester: Carl Ostanek in Kansas; Renée Pellegrino in Florida; Betsy Scott Kimmel in Connecticut; and Kim Couper, Bob Dibble and Kim Nussbaum-Jones, who are current or former United Airlines employees who helped me with that angle. Ryan Westphal, an assistant professor of economics at Brandeis University (and a nephew-in-law), gave me a quick, but comforting, sanity check for my crude effort to quantify the odds of any random person being the Chester I was searching for. Anne Blythe, a journalist formerly with *The News & Observer* and now a contributor to *The Assembly,* and two linguistics scholars at the University of North Carolina at Chapel Hill, Brian Hsu and Paul Roberge, helped me wrestle with one of the story's most perplexing questions: did Chester's mother work for United Airlines.

In the original version of these Acknowledgements, I somehow failed to thank Nicole Pajor Moore for her skillful work in compiling all of the Facebook posts into an attractive, hard-copy volume of her design. Thanks also to Marc Maximov, who produced the audiobook.

My three sisters, Isabel, Carter and Marty, read various drafts and then shared the Facebook posts with their far larger networks of Facebook friends. Marty even showed me how to upload a photo to my very first call-to-action Facebook post. That I had not ever done so before shows how much of a Facebook neophyte I was. My wife and daughter also made many helpful suggestions, even while suffering through my months-long obsession with finding Chester.

I spoke with four members of Chester's family, including his son Doug. I reached out to Chester's other surviving child, a daughter, but never heard from her. The Pratt family members I connected with were unfailingly gracious and trusting. I promised that I would remove any information for which they were the source, and to which they objected; the only detail that was left out of the Facebook posts, at their request, was a fun fact regarding Taylor Swift, which I had alluded to in Chapter 6 but deliberately never revisited. Two of Doug's first cousins, Rev. Dorrie Pratt and Nancy Ellis, generously shared photos of Chester Pratt and other members of the Pratt family – for which I'm grateful.

Before my father's sudden death, I was hopeful that he and I would meet Doug Pratt and other members of the extended Pratt family in person. Doug ran a business in Boone, North Carolina, for many years and now lives in South Carolina. Doug's cousin Dorrie lives in Knoxville, Tennessee, and told me she plans to retire within the next few years and move to the Research Triangle Park area in North Carolina, where I live. During my search for Chester, I also discovered that another of Doug's cousins, Sara Boshart, lived at the time just a mile and a half from Dad's condo in Raleigh – a small world coincidence that thrilled him.

Sadly, the much-anticipated dinner with me and my father and Sara and her husband John, and my sister Isabel, never happened; it had been scheduled for what turned out to be the day after Dad's funeral. Isabel and I have since gotten together with Sara and John – we met for dinner, and I proudly wore Dad's Carolina blue blazer. We all agreed that a reunion of the Pratt and Worthy families would be a fitting coda to this story.

For now, I'll end with a prayer that Dorrie, an Episcopal priest, sent me. She and I had several email exchanges as I neared the end of my search for her Uncle Buster. In one email, she wrote: "On behalf of our family, thank you for helping us learn about these incredible people that we knew as grandparents and uncle or dad but never heard their backstories. Unfortunately, much was never said in our family and details of lives not disclosed. We are indebted to your dad and you."

In a separate email, she shared the following:

Dear Ford,

Thank you, what an incredible story of a brief encounter so many years ago between our families.

I have been wanting to share this prayer with you and your Dad. I wrote it for a World War II veteran in my parish in North Carolina to share with all the veterans from Franklin who were traveling to Washington, DC on an Honor Flight. It was originally written around 2008 or so.

Veterans Prayer

Almighty God, we give you thanks
for the brave men and women
who have valiantly served this country,
risking life and limb for our freedom.
They continue to teach the world
about selfless service, honor, integrity and fidelity.

We pray, O Lord, that the world never forgets the cost of war
and the brave souls who rise to the call
to strive for freedom for all.
May they know our never-ending gratitude.
And may the world learn to live in Your love,
so perhaps, one day, we will live in peace and harmony —
and Your Kingdom will reign on the earth.
Amen.

Thank you for your service.

Dorrie ended her note with this message:

"I pray your Dad has a wonderful birthday celebration."

It felt like a blessing for more than just a birthday – a quiet grace note at the end of a long journey. And the perfect note to end on.

About the Author

A longtime North Carolinian, Ford S. Worthy was born in Charlotte, grew up in Raleigh and attended the University of North Carolina at Chapel Hill, graduating with a Bachelor of Arts degree in Interdisciplinary Studies. He worked as a researcher and writer for *Fortune* magazine in New York and later served as the magazine's bureau chief in Chicago and Hong Kong. His article "The Coming Defaults in Junk Bonds" was selected as a finalist for the National Magazine Award in 1988. Following his time at *Fortune*, he earned a law degree from the University of Chicago, where he was a member of the *University of Chicago Law Review*. He worked as an attorney in Raleigh before joining Pappas Capital, a biotech venture capital firm in Durham. He has served as a partner, and now senior advisor, at Pappas Capital since 1997, and is a senior advisor and board member for North Carolina Longform Magazine, publisher of *The Assembly*. He and his wife Allison live in Chapel Hill.

InSearchOfChester.com

www.ingramcontent.com/pod-product-compliance
Lightning Source LLC
Chambersburg PA
CBHW051634120626
46551CB00014B/2077